M000265997

The Struggles of Identity, Education, and Agency in the Lives of Undocumented Students

Rick —
Keep that spirit
alive and resist!
♡ BM.

Aurora Chang

The Struggles of Identity, Education, and Agency in the Lives of Undocumented Students

The Burden of Hyperdocumentation

palgrave
macmillan

Aurora Chang
School of Education
Loyola University School of Education
Chicago, Illinois, USA

ISBN 978-3-319-64613-8   ISBN 978-3-319-64614-5   (eBook)
https://doi.org/10.1007/978-3-319-64614-5

Library of Congress Control Number: 2017954577

© The Editor(s) (if applicable) and The Author(s) 2018
This work is subject to copyright. All rights are solely and exclusively licensed by the Publisher, whether the whole or part of the material is concerned, specifically the rights of translation, reprinting, reuse of illustrations, recitation, broadcasting, reproduction on microfilms or in any other physical way, and transmission or information storage and retrieval, electronic adaptation, computer software, or by similar or dissimilar methodology now known or hereafter developed.
The use of general descriptive names, registered names, trademarks, service marks, etc. in this publication does not imply, even in the absence of a specific statement, that such names are exempt from the relevant protective laws and regulations and therefore free for general use.
The publisher, the authors and the editors are safe to assume that the advice and information in this book are believed to be true and accurate at the date of publication. Neither the publisher nor the authors or the editors give a warranty, express or implied, with respect to the material contained herein or for any errors or omissions that may have been made. The publisher remains neutral with regard to jurisdictional claims in published maps and institutional affiliations.

Cover image © Gabe Palmer / Alamy Stock Photo

Printed on acid-free paper

This Palgrave Macmillan imprint is published by Springer Nature
The registered company is Springer International Publishing AG
The registered company address is: Gewerbestrasse 11, 6330 Cham, Switzerland

I dedicate this book to my first teachers, mi mama, Peppina Liano, y mi papa, Jorge Arturo Chang.

PREFACE

This book is a personal and academic pursuit. It weaves together two distinct and powerfully related sources of knowledge: (1) my journey/transition from a once undocumented immigrant from Guatemala to a hyperdocumented academic and (2) years of ongoing national research on the identity, education, and agency of undocumented college students. In interlacing both my personal experiences with findings from my empirical qualitative research, I explore practical and theoretical pedagogical, curricular, and policy-related discussions around issues that impact undocumented immigrants while providing compelling rich narrative vignettes (both personal and from my study participants). Collectively, these findings support my overall argument that undocumented students can cultivate an empowering self-identity by performing the role of infallible cultural citizen.

In many ways, all people from marginalized groups can relate to the idea of hyperdocumentation as it has been a historical practice—this notion of having to "show our papers" in various iterations to prove our identity but more so to prove our human worthiness. The idea of "showing one's papers" has a chilling history, taking us back to places and times we never want to repeat: Nazi roundups, the racial sorting of apartheid South Africa, and the practices of the Soviet empire. Requiring papers—like those that might be required for admission to vote—echoes the poll taxes and literacy tests in the Jim Crow South, as well as recent voting requirements, used to keep black voters from exercising their freedom. Targeting the so-called undocumented is hardly a new phenomenon.

In the United States, the groups of people targeted as such are simply a moving target at the whim of political inclinations.

This book is a combination of previously published journal articles and new material that follow a somewhat unconventional approach to academic writing. In all my writing endeavors, I have always worked to weave narrative and experiential knowledge into academic conventions—this has not been easy but I hope it will make the reading of this book more engaging and accessible. The truth is that academic writing, as it is currently understood and taught, will never be for the masses, but my small wish is that this work inches a bit closer to that end. There is no greater form of flattery than when a high school student will write to me and share how much they could relate to something I wrote. That tells me that, to some degree, my writing is relevant, readable, and authentic. If you have ever worked with high school students, you know that they call things as they see them.

This book was written for those students, teachers, and scholars who: (1) identify as, study, want to learn about, and/or work with undocumented people; (2) have been trained to take the "I" out of their writing for fear that it would be deemed biased, subjective, lacking in rigor, political, narcissistic, unacceptable, or worthless; (3) understand the revolutionary power in centering experiential knowledge as official knowledge; (4) need models as to how to write themselves and people from marginalized populations and their counterstories into academia; and (5) would like advice as to how to work with undocumented students.

This book was written for every undocumented person who has ever been unable to find the language to express their realities. It was written to honor my parents and their journey of immigration that continues today. It was written for my siblings who each, in their own way, has narrated the story of their lives built on the sacrifices, intellects, and bodies of those before us. It was written for every teacher who saw the potential in this little brown girl and for every person who expected the opposite. Finally, it was written for that same five-year-old immigrant girl with big dreams and often debilitating anxiety. I hold that five-year-old tightly, mightily, and with every assurance that I am with her.

This book is divided into seven chapters.

In the first chapter, I discuss how my positionality impacts my epistemology, specifically through my rationale for pursuing a profession as an academic. I begin the book from this angle because why I chose academia directly relates to the notion that I introduce and emphasize so strongly in this book—*hyperdocumentation*. I discuss my love of educational spaces and how they served as safe havens for me and how I nurtured and honed particular academic skills, such as writing, to inhabit privileged worlds that I would otherwise lack access to. I entertain the idea of being an activist scholar that works within and without academia to participate in nonviolent resistance, manifested in daily acts of disobedience.

In the second chapter, "Undocumented to Hyperdocumented: A Jornada of Papers, Protection, and PhD Status," I situate my own positionality as a once undocumented Guatemalan immigrant. I describe my experience of hyperdocumentation—the effort to accrue awards, accolades, and eventually academic degrees to compensate for my undocumented status. In spite of my visible successes and naturalization, I discuss how I still confront the rage and intolerance of American "commonsense" beliefs about immigration. My narrative questions the pursuit of documentation as a means to legitimacy and acceptance in American society. This introduction lays the foundation for my argument and outlines the chapters to follow.

In the third chapter, "Privileged and Undocumented: Toward a Borderland Love Ethic," I further explore my positionality, moving from the personal to the academic as I discuss the tensions of what it means to be a "deserving" native researcher. In this way, I present my conceptual framework from which my writing stems and offer a theoretical situatedness as researcher. I begin by experimenting with the meaning of a *borderland love ethic* as a theoretical framework that centers on nurturing our strength to love in spaces of contention, tolerance of ambiguity as a revolutionary virtue, and humbly beginning anew again and again. Drawing from an extended interview with a participant of a larger study about undocumented students, I describe our positionalities with respect to privilege and undocumented status as the central foci. I use my own dilemma of understanding and reconciling my position as a once undocumented immigrant to a now hyperdocumented (Chang 2011) native researcher, studying undocumented people, to work through the possibility of a borderland love ethic. Relying primarily on the theoretical works of Anzaldúa (1987), Darder (2003), and hooks (2000), I ask, how we, as scholars, enact love in our research amidst our seemingly contradictory positions of oppression and privilege. I contend that one possibility is by employing a borderland love ethic that embraces ambiguity, rejects binary positions, and humbly acknowledges our constant state of arriving, both as researchers and participants.

In the fourth chapter, "Figured Worlds and American Dreams: An Exploration of Agency and Identity Among Undocumented Students," I begin reporting on one of my studies of undocumented students with a focus on identity, education, and agency. The lives of undocumented students are at the mercy of the political ups and downs that impact their daily realities. No matter the agentic acts these students take to reach their goals or steps they take to simply survive, there is a limit to what they can achieve in the context of the law. While the unpredictable journey of the DREAM (Development, Relief, and Education for Alien Minors) Act, which sought a conditional pathway to citizenship, raised students' hopes since its inception in 2001, xenophobic messages about undocumented immigrants stealing American jobs, committing crimes, and otherwise abusing the US system of government continue to proliferate. These symbolically violent messages depict undocumented people as uneducated and deficient—as takers of what is not theirs, bringing with them problems rather than contributions.

As a result, undocumented students find themselves on continuously shifting ground, calibrating each decision they make in accordance with or as a strategic reaction to the existing political climate. Specifically, some undocumented students find themselves in an ongoing internal battle to fashion an identity that counters the pervasive stereotypes of undocumented people through a process of hyperdocumentation (Chang 2011), while simultaneously bearing the weight of fierce anti-immigrant sentiment. In this chapter, I ask the following questions: How do undocumented students navigate educational spaces? In what ways do their legal statuses impact the production of their identities? How do they exert agency within the parameters of their undocumented status? In answering these questions, I explore the ways in which some undocumented students *figure*—or take agency in shaping meaning of—their worlds, find identity in their education, and leverage community cultural wealth (Yosso 2005) as a source of critical hope and resilience in their quest to achieve the ever-nebulous American Dream.

In the fifth chapter, "Doing Good and Doing Damage: Educators' Impact on Undocumented Latinx Students' Lives," I explore educators' particularly poignant role in impacting undocumented students' lives. I draw from the perspectives of undocumented students to examine how educators impact undocumented Latinx lives for better or for worse. I focus on undocumented Latinx students' perceptions of educators' everyday interactions with them and use Valenzuela's (1999) notions of educación and authentic caring to analyze how students make meaning of them. I stress the significance of interactions that do good and others that do damage and suggest that educators can powerfully influence the lives of undocumented youth through small, even momentary interactions.

Studying the impact of educators' actions and omissions from the vantage point of undocumented students is critical to informing current practices, behaviors, and interventions. This chapter attempts to begin a conversation around the role of educators in undocumented students' lives by asking: How do undocumented students perceive their everyday interactions with educators? Of these interactions, which ones do students identify as "doing good" and "doing damage"? In this chapter, I argue that individual educators have the power to "do good" or "do damage" in the lives of undocumented youth. I analyze, discuss, and present implications about the impact of educators on undocumented students, noting that the actions and omissions of individual educators can have lasting effects on their lives.

This chapter reveals "children who have been raised to dream, yet are cut off from the very mechanisms that allow them to achieve their dreams" (Gonzales 2009, p. 6); their dreams are tempered and even squashed by limited educational opportunities, low academic expectations, fear of deportation, inability to acquire employment, and mental health challenges associated with the stress of being undocumented. In the midst of such adversity, undocumented students pointed to human mechanisms that can serve as gateways or gatekeepers for the futures of undocumented students; those human mechanisms are educators.

In the sixth chapter, I offer my thoughts around academy agency and the burden of perfectionism that undocumented students face. I solidify my argument that some undocumented students can cultivate an empowering self-identity by performing the role of infallible cultural citizen. Drawing from the borderland love ethic framework, I conclude by reconnecting my own personal experiences as once undocumented to now hyperdocumented immigrant to those of the participants, drawing conclusions and posing questions for the reader to ponder.

In the seventh chapter, I get practical, providing advice for those who work with undocumented students. Drawing on conversations with undocumented students, I present three major pieces of advice as directly shared with me: (1) You don't need to know a lot to help me; (2) Don't tell me everything is going to be alright; and (3) Walk the path alongside me. I suggest that while we must keep the larger political arena on the forefront, engage tirelessly in our fight to battle draconian immigration policies, we must also stay present on the now, mindfully focusing on the everyday impact we can have on undocumented students' lives through our interactions with them. Rather than fall into a pit of despair by succumbing to the grandiosity of global politics where we often feel powerless, we can look at our own contexts and find ways to enact agency within our locus of control. Finally, I encourage readers to write themselves into academia by defining what that means and explaining how I wrote myself into academia throughout this process.

Chicago, IL USA   Aurora Chang

REFERENCES

Anzaldúa, G. (1987). *Borderlands: La frontera – The new mestiza*. San Francisco: Aunt Lute Books.

Chang, A. (2011). Undocumented to hyperdocumented: A jornada of protection, papers, and PhD status. *Harvard Educational Review, 81*(3), 508–520.

Darder, A. (2003). Teaching as an act of love: Reflections on Paulo Freire and his contributions to our lives and our work. In A. Darder, M. Baltodano & R. D. Torres (Eds.), *The critical pedagogy reader*. New York: Routledge.

Gonzales, R. (2009). *Special report: Young lives on hold: The college dreams of undocumented students* (pp. 1–27). The College Board.

hooks, b. (2000). *All about love*. New York: First Perennial.

Yosso, T. J. (2005). Whose culture has capital? A critical race theory discussion of community cultural wealth. *Race, Ethnicity, and Education, 8*(1), 69–91.

Valenzuela, A. (1999). *Subtractive schooling: U.S.-Mexican youth and the politics of caring*. Albany: State University of New York Press.

ACKNOWLEDGMENTS

I want to thank the amazing people in my life who have supported me along this road. Inevitably, I will overlook someone, but you all know who you are.

The first people I need to acknowledge are my parents, Peppina Liano and Jorge Arturo Chang. I have borne witness to your struggles and thank you for your sacrifices—those I was privy to and those that you suffered in silence. Your immigration journey, told and untold, has left permanent imprints on my soul. I must also thank my siblings—Blanca, Andres, George, Maria, and, my twinnie, José—who have always supported me in their own ways and made me proud to be a Chang. Todd, my brother-in-law, and Shauna, my sister-in-law—thank you for being there to cheer me on. I must also honor the powerful women in my extended family: Doña Pepa, Silvana Liano, Renata Liano, Doña Celia, and all of the women who have come before me—their struggles and fortitude paved my way. I will always be grateful for my family's unwavering support.

Mamá, you have been my moral compass, my unconditional love, and my inspiration. I witnessed your metamorphosis as a woman, mother, and professional—all of which have left an indelible mark on everything I do. You have been the one and only consistent miracle in my life, fiercely present in my most joyous and painful times. You teach me that every day is better than the last and that we are always arriving. In the end, it is your unfaltering belief and love in me that has carried me through my darkest periods and your unencumbered zest for life that has infused happiness in my proudest moments. I owe everything I am to you.

I also am grateful to the following people that made this book possible:

My dear friends whom I have turned to in different phases of my life for support, laughter, grounding, and compassion—Melissa Martinez, Sonia Cortez, Sabina Neugebauer, AJ Welton, Laura Cortez, Danielle Alsandor, Ingrid Colón, Camille Wilson, Maria Ledesma, Mandeep Birak, Elvira Prieto, Maria Cruz, Sonia Montoya, Bennie Vargas, Gina Coffee, Sergio Delgado, Amy Sarno, Vaughn Beckford, Codi Scott, Peter DeSouza, LaRon Coleman, Alex DeGuia, Vanessa Fonseca, Steve Alvarez, Enrique Romo, Martin Chapa, Lynn Chang, Wayne Enanoria, and Rocio Toriz.

My colleagues who have pushed me, provided me opportunities, and have enthusiastically supported my work—Cheryl Matias, Mark Torrez, Kelly Ferguson, Anita Sagar, LaGarrett King, Cristobal Rodriguez, Joe Saucedo, Paige Gardner, Mark Kucsweski, Karma Chavez, Gabriella Gutierrez y Muhs, Lauren Heidbrink, Juan Carrillo, Dave Stovall, Pam Fenning, Amy Heineke, Mark Engberg, Adam Kennedy, Katherine Kaufka-Walts, Jennifer Esperanza, Adeoye Adeoyome, Tanya Cabrera, Aliza Gilbert, Laura Bohorquez, Ruth Muñoz, Sue Kasun, Lilia Soto, Dolores Cardona, Helen AlaTorre, Corina Lopez, Keith Sturges, Markeeda Newell, Blanca Torres-Olave, Sarita Cohen, Betty Jeanne Taylor, Yvonne Loya, Ryan Miller, and Erin Atwood.

My professional mentors who have exemplified authentic caring through their high expectations, rigorous guidance, generosity, and kindness—Genaro Padilla, Luis Urrieta, Gregory Vincent, Keffrelyn Brown, Anthony Brown, Ann Marie Ryan, Roberto Gonzales, Angela Valenzuela, Kerry Ann Rockquemore, Beth Hatt, Doug Foley, Kevin Foster, Cinthia Salinas, James Montoya, Julian Vasquez Heilig, Victor Saenz, Michael Dantley, David Slavsky, Bridget Kelly, and Lisa Cary.

My teachers, guides, role models, champions, and coaches from afar who have been sources of inspiration and revolutionaries in their own right—Dolores Delgado Bernal, Michael Olivas, Sandra Cisneros, Gloria Anzaldúa, Cherrie Moraga, William Perez, Ana Castillo, Audre Lorde, bell hooks, Gloria Ladson-Billings, Michael Apple, Linda Darling-Hammond, Tara Yosso, Daniel Solorzano, David Takacs, Ruth Behar, Sofia Villenas, Renato Rosaldo, Richard Delgado, Kimberle Crenshaw, Derrick Bell, Paolo Freire, Antonia Darder, Susan B. Coutin, Nicholas DeGenova, Jeffrey Duncan-Andrade, Stella Flores, Leisy Ábrego, Susana Muñoz, Michelle Espino, Lindsay Pérez-Huber, Nel Noddings, Thich Nhat Hanh, Tara Yosso, Sheila Shannon, and Lourdes Diáz Soto.

My students who have been my best teachers and my greatest sources of joy and fulfillment—Amani Edwards, Cristina Rodriguez, Yuliana Rojas, Karla Robles, Esmeralda Rodriguez, Ati Wongsaroj, Carlos Luna, Eyleen Gramajo, Khundmeer Syed, Lisset Larios, Juan Gallegos, Osmar Cruz, Abraham Peña-Talamantes, Zoila Guachichulca, Lucia Peralta, Kidan Araya, Nancy Gutierrez, Tamanisha John, Nico Salas, Jomar Salazar, Anthony Otey, Dominique Clayton, Jose Rivas, Norma Lira, Marlen Nava, Adam Smeets, Yenny Rios, Gam Pham, Danielle Wood, Isaac Hayes, students I taught at Balboa High School, the students I had the privilege of working with in the UC Berkeley Early Academic Outreach Program, all of my Beloit College FYI students and McNair Scholars, the undergraduates I taught at the University of Wyoming, and all of my current students at Loyola University Chicago.

My public school teachers who provided me with so much more than an education; they saw something special in me, nurtured my passion for learning, and taught me to love language—Ms. Landfear, Ms. Forcier, Ms. Garrigan, Ms. McGuire, Mr. Sonagera, Mr. Bauer, Ms. Yamuda, Ms. Galvan, Ms. Johnson, Mrs. Lewis, Mr. Storer, Mr. Boulé, and Mr. Dick.

Finally, let me thank every participant I have ever interviewed in this research. My work rests on your experiences which you so generously shared with me.

[slam papers to floor]
I have a Bachelor's from Berkeley
a Master's from Stanford and
a PhD from the University of Texas at Austin

[bend down to floor to shuffle through papers]
I've written at least 10,000 pages in my lifetime
and will probably reach a million before I'm dead.

[sort through and pass out different papers to people in audience]
I have file cabinets full of papers:
certificates of achievement, perfect attendance awards, straight A report cards, French student of the year, Mathletes winner, Academic Decathlon Finalist, #1 Doubles Tennis Champ, Excellent Citizenship award, applications, forms, personal statements, reference letters, Alumni Scholarship (full ride), Mellon Fellow (full ride), Asian American Award for Leadership, Hispanic Faculty/Staff Association Member of the Year, University Fellowship $50,000

[find CV, reveal it and put it on like a shawl around body]
My CV is 20 pages long
I wear professorial clothes and talk academic talk.
I've done everything I'm supposed to do, right?

But
[stand tall and let the CV shawl fall to the floor, quietly talking aloud]
Yesterday, today, and tomorrow
when I again get confused for a food service worker, hotel staff, or maid—
it's like I
NEVER
EARNED
ANYTHING.

[hands extended to audience]
Don't get me wrong—my father worked coat check at a San Francisco hotel,
my mom sold tamales from our house, I bussed tables to get through school.
It's just that people have no problem assuming that we do THOSE honest
jobs that everyone else WON'T do.
I've just never had someone **accidentally assume** I'm a professor, a doctor,
an author.
You get me?

[Hands in prayer pleading]
Understand that brown skin, prominent nose, black hair, and Mayan
features
TRUMP
21 years of schooling, a prestigious job, and authored articles, chapters, and
books.
I thought my days of fearing everything
as an undocumented "illegal" immigrant from Guatemala were over.
I deluded myself
[collect papers from audience]
thinking that I had hyperdocumented my way out of racism, sexism, hetero-
normativity, classism, ableism, ageism, and xenophobia.

[tone gets powerful, holding papers close to chest, on heart]
I'm a writer
I'm a scholar
And a professor at Loyola University
but you wouldn't know that.
Would you?

CONTENTS

LIST OF TABLE

CHAPTER 1

Introduction

My personal life and my academic life are not separate; they never have been. This book is no different. Who I am as an academic is deeply personal and it is this intimacy that weaves these pages together. This book is somewhat nostalgic, rigorously reflective, and always vulnerable. It is with a mix of excitement, responsibility, and apprehension that I present it. The excitement comes from the newness and surrealism of a first book. The responsibility comes from the obligation I have to share my research about undocumented students and my privilege in engaging in such a historically exclusive activity. The apprehension comes from the risk of sharing too much information—permanently. There is something about writing a book that comes as close to truth-telling as one can get and that feels heavy because you want to get it "right." But, as I have learned, there is no such thing as "pure" knowledge; all knowledge passes through a filter of subjectivities and positionalities. So-called objectivity meets its limits through the permeable fibers of the author's filter. Understanding this permeability is central to the consumption of knowledge; it dictates the manner in which you ingest information and how you approach its analysis.

Who we are, how we are positioned, and how we position ourselves within our worlds shape what we write about and how we write about it. As Takacs (2003) notes, in one of my favorite articles, *How Does Your Positionality Bias Your Epistemology*:

© The Author(s) 2018
A. Chang, *The Struggles of Identity, Education, and Agency in the Lives of Undocumented Students*,
https://doi.org/10.1007/978-3-319-64614-5_1

> Simply acknowledging that one's views are not inevitable—that one's posi-
> tionality can bias one's epistemology—is itself a leap for many people, one
> that can help make us more open to the world's possibilities. When we
> develop the skill of understanding how we know what we know, we acquire
> a key to lifelong learning. When we teach this skill, we help students sample
> the rigors and delights of the examined life. When we ask students to learn to
> think for themselves and to understand themselves as thinkers—rather than
> telling them what to think and have them recite it back—we can help foster
> habits of introspection, analysis, and open, joyous communication. (p. 28)

In some instances, how one's positionality impacts one's epistemology is
somewhat straightforward, like my positionality as a once undocumented
immigrant writing about undocumented immigrants. My positionality,
the multiple social identities, and unique experiences that situate me as a
once undocumented immigrant inform my epistemology, how I come to
view and make meaning of knowledge. In other instances, an author's
writing topic may seem neutral but you only need to peel back a few layers
to understand that all writing comes from a personal place. As Takacs
(2003) points out, "knowledge does not arrive unmediated from the
world; rather knowledge gets constructed by interaction between the
questioner and the world" (p. 31). I dare you to come up with one author
whose writing isn't at all tied to who they are; some of us just choose to
be explicit about this connection.

So, I am inviting you into an aspect of my world, knowing that there is
some vulnerability involved. As Ruth Behar (1997) tells us:

> Writing vulnerably takes as much skill, nuance, and willingness to follow
> through on all the ramifications of a complicated idea as does writing invul-
> nerably and distantly. I would say it takes yet greater skill. The worst that can
> happen in an invulnerable text is that it will be boring. But when the author
> has made herself or himself vulnerable, the stakes are higher: a boring self-
> revelation, one that fails to move the reader, is more than embarrassing; it is
> humiliating. (pp. 13–14)

So, while my writing carries some risk—the possibility that I will embarrass
myself by producing a less than moving self-revelation, for example—I
believe that the benefit of encouraging other scholars, especially those
from marginalized backgrounds, to write themselves into academia, out-
weighs any possible humiliation. I thank you for taking the time to get to
know me and my work. It is easy to sail adrift in the exclusive world of

academia, research, and writing. By reading this work, you provide me with an anchor, a reminder to keep this work relevant and rigorous. You give me a reason to keep on writing.

In academia, we often get lost in our own bubble of language, prestige, recognition, and competition. Particularly, as scholars of marginalized identities, we grapple with the tension of serving the immediate needs of communities we so deeply care about and jumping through the requisite hoops of publishing, producing, teaching, and servicing. In writing this book, I have had the opportunity to reflect on why I chose to pursue an academic career.

I think this is an important place to start because why I chose academia directly relates to the notion that I introduce and emphasize so strongly in this book—hyperdocumentation. Hyperdocumentation is a person's excessive production of documents, texts, and papers in an effort to compensate for a feeling of unworthiness. In my context, I hyperdocumented in an attempt to compensate for my undocumented immigrant status. In many ways, I still do. Even though I am now technically an American citizen, my identity of being once undocumented, apart from the privileges that I now enjoy as an officiated legal immigrant, will always be with me, along with all of the associated behaviors that went along with that status. Arriving to academia was not a straight and narrow path nor one that I chose blindly. In fact, I pretty much resisted it from the start. I was a high school teacher in the San Francisco Bay Area, program coordinator at the University of California at Berkeley, educational manager at the College Board, student affairs administrator at the University of Texas at Austin, and director of the McNair Scholars Program at Beloit College before this phase in my life, opting for the practical, on the ground, "in the trenches" kind of work. But even before my work life began, I was a seemingly simple immigrant kid going to and from school, doing home-work, chores, going to mass and playing, thinking about how I couldn't wait to grow up—life seemed so slow then. Now, my life can't seem to slow down enough; instead, it is filled with compounding deadlines, appointments and multi-technological communications with a pace that I could have hardly understood as a child.

I never once imagined that I would be a professor at a prestigious university when I was in my early years of schooling, college, or even during my master's program. I always pictured professors in white—white skinned in white lab coats writing on white boards and going home to white picket fences. Instead, I convinced myself that I would use my academic pedigree to, as we say in the world of student affairs, to engage in "direct service" with students. I was not cut out to live what I envisioned as a solitary "life of the mind" nor did I see myself as at all worthy of professorship. While I knew I was good at doing school, the prospects of professor-hood never made it into the archives of my imagination. It simply seemed unrealistic. The only reason I ended up in academia was because I saw other women of color, like me, doing it and, like many others before me and alongside of me, I was encouraged to apply to a doctoral program by a couple of professors of color who basically "gave me the tap" and convinced me that it would be irresponsible of me not to use my talents in academia. Do you know how many people would dream of a job like this? Think of all the folks that haven't had your same opportunities. You're a gifted writer—don't waste your skills away. Do it because you CAN. I was "obligated" into the profession; those professors, like Dr. Luis Urrieta and Dr. Gregory Vincent, knew me well—that Catholic guilt worked on me every time, not to mention my mama, who has always had incredibly high expectations and aspirations of me. What once seemed like a faraway institution only meant as a place for me to learn and be taught became an office in Chicago's Lewis Towers with a name placard that reads Dra. Aurora Chang, where I teach courses, counsel students, conduct research, and write effusively. In retrospect, this career choice should come as no surprise to me. As it turns out, educational spaces have always been the spaces where I have felt most protected, most safe, most alive.

It is important to understand that I fit the trope of "deserving immigrant" and so do the undocumented students whom I have focused on in this book. We got straight A's, maintained clean criminal records, held leadership positions, participated in the capitalist myth of meritocracy, and performed good cultural citizenry. Roberto Gonzales (2016) calls this phenomenon, "the slippery slope of deservingness" (p. 218). He notes:

> For many immigration restrictionists, 'illegal is illegal' and there should be no shades of gray. But as immigration debates have heated up and legislative attempts have stalled, advocates have resorted to rhetorical measures and the promotion of policies that draw attention to two types of immigrants: those who deserve to be in the United States and those who do not. (p. 219)

He goes on to emphasize that "as long as there is an 'undeserving' category, there is always a risk that a random event or a change in the political tide can shift the discourse to cast all immigrants as undeserving" (p. 219).

He stresses that it is easy to have sympathy for "innocent" children that are only in this country because of their parents' "sins" but that these children grow up and then what? This book is not about pitting some groups of immigrants against others or holding these particular undocumented immigrants as exceptional immigrants that somehow are more deserving than others. Rather, this book focuses on a small group of academically successful undocumented immigrants' experiences of hyperdocumentation. If anything, their stories further support the slippery slope theory since their positive school experiences fail to guarantee citizenship.

As you will see in the chapters that follow, educational spaces have always been havens of mind, body, and spirit for me. As a shy immigrant girl from a chaotic and ultimately instrumental household, classroom walls provided the kind of control and structure that relieved my anxiety and allowed me to carve out a neat, warm, and safe space—one where I didn't necessarily have to share tight quarters, facilitate grown-up arguments, attend to adult matters, or feel scared of what a bad mood might bring. At school, I forged my own identity. I was the first grader that showed up to class with anxiety-induced stomachaches every morning, hoping my teacher would take pity on me by isolating me in a reading corner or send me to the heavenly nurse's office where I could lay on the little couch, stare at the popcorn ceiling, and daydream all by myself. I was the seven-year-old that wrote short stories about Armageddon, causing my teacher to individually pull me aside (something I loved) and ask if anything was wrong at home. I was the quiet girl with the bowl haircut that made friends with all the outsiders—the "weird" kids that didn't fit in. Perhaps that made me one of them. At school, I knew exactly what to do. I had the routine down.

At home, my only goal was to be a quintessential "good girl." Within my Guatemalan, Catholic upbringing, this meant two things—be obedient and be quiet. I savored every minute I spent in the kitchen with Mati, what we used to call my mom. I was her right hand—helping to make daily breakfast for the eight of us, setting the table and washing dishes, rolling out masa for empanadas, turning the wooden spoon in circles in the pan of refried black beans until the consistency was just right. We seemed to use up ingredients as quickly as we bought them. Trips to Costco were a weekly occurrence with a flatbed cart stocked high with rolls of toilet paper, gallons of milk, boxes of cereal, and the occasional pair of shoes or jacket that one of the kids might need.

Nothing satisfied me more than pleasing my parents and teachers. In a household of eight, the six of us kids could barely get a word in edgewise with our parents—there was simply not enough time in a day. Each of us had a different strategy for accessing our parents' scarce and golden attention. My academic prowess was my victorious way of earning that small but significant piece of attention. Kids at school thought they were teasing me by calling me a "teacher's pet"; little did they know how much I relished that unintended accolade. It didn't take much to fill me with joy hidden behind an awkward smile. I was a pretty serious kid and little crooked smiles were about as much excitement as I could muster at any given time. My academic life was the one thing that made everything in my life feel stable and secure. As long as my standing at school was good, so were all of my important relationships. It is rare to find even one thing in life that makes you feel secure—school was that blanket for me.

Religion was another source of security, albeit temporary. I grew up in a very Latino Catholic household. My parents went to daily mass and were part of a prelature of the Catholic Church called Opus Dei, an organization now made famous and fictionalized by *The Da Vinci Code*. Our life as an Opus Dei family is the subject for an entirely separate book project, but I raise it in this context because it paints a fuller picture of my upbringing and, more specifically, it might explain part of my fixation on being infallible. In Opus Dei, we were taught to be "saintly" by living ordinary lives—perfectly. As an adolescent, at the age of 13, I "whistled"—this is what Opus Dei used to call it when people responded to the vocational call of numerary (in its simplest explanation, the equivalent of a lay nun). For five years, I took the vows of celibacy and poverty. It was during those critical years of development where I became obsessed with the idea of perfection—spiritually, physically, and academically. The "spiritual formation" I received during this period of my life laid the foundation for my dispositions of obedience, humility, and sacrifice. At the age of 18, I left or, rather, escaped. While I physically left the organization, its imprints remain with me. The restraint it required for me to reign in temptations of the flesh as an adolescent is the same discipline I now draw from to survive the endurance required of writing.

While academic achievement, in general, was critical in shaping my identity, the idea of perfectionism was even more powerful. Being saintly or perfect not only promised worldly satisfactions, it also ensured rewards beyond this life. My attachment to being a perfect child was tied to notions of heaven, spirituality, and the divine. Undoubtedly, this mania informed my gnawing need to perform flawlessness. There was nothing quite as powerful as knowing that I had seemingly found the key to all that was good. This also created a bit of neediness in me, a desire to be recognized for my hard work, discipline, and virtuousness: something I was able to satisfy through a particularly valuable academic skill—writing.

From the time I can remember, I grasped the power of good writing. From a young age, I wrote short stories, poetry, book reports, and essays that were always incredibly meaningful for me. They allowed me to inhabit worlds that I could not physically occupy. It was my therapy, my best friend, and my comfort. What could happen to me in the exquisite seclusion of white pages and black ink? Writing was always that quiet space, that room of my own that I longed for growing up. And while writing was indeed a relatively private act, it also served as a public and vocally silent unveiling of who I was—a way of saying, I'm here, look at me, pay attention to me, love me. This is how my love affair with writing began and the way it continues to unfold. This is important because many times, budding graduate students or thoughtful undergraduates will ask me, "how do I know that being in academia is right for me?" There are a variety of possible responses but the one that I seem to repeat most often is this, "Let me ask you this. Do you feel that you must write, that you might die if you don't?" I deeply believe that a happy life in academia stems from a direct correlation between filling that gap between what you love artistically and what you need to do as a social activist. You must love to write, and even more so, writing must be a survival mechanism. I get pushback at times from colleagues about this advice, reminding me that writing is a science as much as it is an art form, that this might discourage some amazing folks from pursuing academia. But, I stand by it because you have to honor writing like you would a partner. It is a relationship built on kindness, passion, commitment, and perseverance. You can't enter the relationship naively without knowing how much work it will be and how consuming it can be.

I am also not a traditional scholar as far as my approach to writing is concerned. The writing that has always moved me has been biographical to some extent. There is something so comforting and affirming about an author's vulnerability, especially when it has spoken to my own experiences or, even more powerfully, has reflected my experiences. James Baldwin said it so perfectly:

> You think your pain and your heartbreak are unprecedented in the history
> of the world, but then you read. It was books that taught me that the things
> that tormented me most were the very things that connected me with all the
> people who were alive, who had ever been alive.

When you see yourself in the written word, you are born. Your reality is named. Your existence is confirmed. The power of documenting one's experience lies in the corporeality of text. This sentiment takes me back to De Anza High School in Richmond, California. I clearly remember sitting in my AP (Advanced Placement) History class as a junior. Mr. Atwood was giving one of his lectures on democracy. It occurred to me that I had never read anything about Latinos in my US history textbooks. I wondered if we existed. Why did my family immigrate here? Who else had immigrated here? How did we fit into American history? It wasn't until my freshman year at UC Berkeley that I took my first Chicano Studies class, met fellow Latino peers, and became politically aware that I began to understand. It's not that we hadn't been here; it was that we hadn't been written into history or rather that whoever wrote these books did not write us into history. Such an omission made me feel alone, unaccounted for, dismissed, and disposable. Not only was my history not represented in a textbook but most of the authors I was exposed to were white. This sent a clear message to me—I was alive but I didn't matter enough to be inscribed in text.

It was also in college that I read my first book by a Latina author, Gloria Anzaldúa. *Borderlands La Frontera* changed my life. Anzaldúa was the first person whom I had ever read that intertwined her own lived experiences with theorizing. She was also the first non-fiction author who didn't quote any other scholars. It was as if her writing stood alone, like she dared to speak without some old white guy validating her words. There was nothing pretentious or false about the conventions she adhered to, the struggle she spoke, the anguished liberation she felt. Who was this bold queer Chicana spitting it in Spanglish, unapologetically telling her truths, naming her shames, and divulging her secrets? She made me see:

> I am visible—see this Indian face—yet I am invisible. I both blind them with
> my beak nose and am their blind spot. But I exist, we exist. They'd like to
> think I have melted in the pot. But I haven't. We haven't. (p. 108)

Her writing animated mine.

Since then, it has always been my goal to make the personal, academic. In other words, I privilege experiential knowledge as official knowledge. So, I guess some would say that I engage in "me-search." This is the idea that academics write about themselves in a belly-gazing sort of fashion, the utmost act of pompous self-adoration often implicated as less than rigorous research. I love this cynicism because addressing it involves the unpacking of several notions, one of which is what counts as official knowledge. It also has much to do with the idea of positionality—the ways in which some people are deemed already subjective or rather unobjective because of their marginalized identities. Doesn't your background as a person of color make you biased toward writing about people of color? In other words, the assumption is that my "insider" status will somehow contaminate the otherwise object way that people with my similar backgrounds could be studied. White academics are not questioned about how their cultural background biases their research because whiteness and white academics are, by default, neutral and normal. In fact, white scholars are not only *not* questioned about the validity of their research but are set on a pedestal when they study issues that are about people of color; they are especially praised for the heroic, worthy, and selfless work they engage in. By writing myself into academia, I resist such irrationality and white supremacist ideology. I testify to those ancestors of ours who were never allowed to write, criminalized for being literate and daring to incorporate themselves into history.

At the same time, I am cognizant of tension that exists as an academic activist. At the end of a recent talk at a Midwestern university, I was asked, "So, do you consider your work to be activist work? If so, can you explain to me how you can both work within an oppressive system while being against it?" It was a question that triggered all of my insecurities and misgivings of having chosen this route. It is no secret that academia is a space of exclusivity, white supremacy, and hegemony. It is also, however, a ripe space for minute acts of powerful agency and filled with openings for tireless disobedience. For those of us who consider ourselves activists, the space of academia is not for the faint of heart. Yet there is one thing that I know for sure—my path to this book is one paved with the steps of undocumented people globally. The ability to write this book is a testament to the inspiration, fortitude, and resolve that embodies immigrants everywhere. I am forever connected to those border-crossers, nation-builders, and dream-makers/keepers who prize the ultimate form of capital—hope.

If you haven't already done so, write about your story, your family's story, or your community's story. I don't believe in coincidences, only in serendipity. Let this be my gentle tap on your shoulder, encouraging you to tell it—whatever it may be for you. As Davalos (2008) so astutely notes in her piece, *Sin Vergüenza: Chicana Feminist Theorizing*, when relaying her elation at receiving a rejection letter from a journal which demanded as a condition of consideration for publication that she "write herself back into her analysis" (p. 151), she felt as if she "had found a home in feminist scholarship because clarification of the author's standpoint or positionality was fundamental, an essential aspect of theory-making" (p. 151). Write yourself into academia. I know it's hard and seemingly impossible at times.

> trying to convince myself
> i am allowed
> to take up space
> is like writing with
> my left hand
> when i was born
> to use my right
> -*the idea of shrinking is hereditary*
> (Kaur, 2014 p. 29)

You are allowed to take up space. You do not need to shrink. You are not alone. Someone is waiting to connect to your story. Your story is waiting to be told.

REFERENCES

Anzaldúa, G. (1987). *Borderlands La Frontera: The New Mestiza*. San Francisco: Aunt Lute Books.

Baldwin, J. (1985). A talk to teachers. In *The price of the ticket, collected non-fiction 1948–1985*. New York: St. Martin's Press.

Behar, R. (1997). *The vulnerable observer: Anthropology that breaks your heart*. Boston: Beacon Press.

Davalos, K. M. (2008). Sin Verguenza: Chicana feminist theorizing. *Feminist Studies, 34*(1/2), 151–171.

Gonzales, R. (2016). *Lives in Limbo: Undocumented and coming of age in America*. Berkeley: University of California Press.

Kaur, R. (2014). *Milk and honey*. Kansas City: Andrews McMeel Publishing.

Takacs, D. (2003). How does your positionality bias your epistemology? *Thought & Action: The NEA Higher Education Journal, 19*(1), 27–38.

CHAPTER 2

Undocumented to Hyperdocumented: A Jornada of Papers, Protection, and PhD Status

I clearly remember myself as a young, brown Guatemalan girl, going with my family on our routine trips to the chained-to-the-floor plastic chairs, standing in line for the next available window, and having a "Next, may I help you?" government worker assist us. On the surface, it appeared as if we were part of a discrete and mundane series of tasks in the precise ritual of obtaining our sacrosanct green cards. Yet, the thought of acquiring *papeles* was anything but mundane: acquiring papers was synonymous with achieving the American Dream.

In many ways, the process was religious. We followed the INS[1] doctrine and performed processional rites—all culminating in a repentant return to an imagined place of social acceptance and redemption from illegal immigration. We hoped that, after following certain commandments (such as passing the citizenship test, following federal immigration rules, and waiting), the pearly gates of the United States would open wide for us prodigal children. In preparation for our INS visits, our parents would force us into our Sunday best—thin white socks with lace trim and white patent-leather Mary Janes for the girls and blue suits and shiny, tight black shoes for the boys. And none of us was exempt from Dippity-do, the revered hair gel

This chapter as article was originally published in 2011 and is reprinted with permission given by the publishers (Chang 2011).

© The Author(s) 2018
A. Chang, *The Struggles of Identity, Education, and Agency in the Lives of Undocumented Students,*
https://doi.org/10.1007/978-3-319-64614-5_2

that came in a vat from the Mexican *tienda* and that was saved for special occasions such as these. The rigid seating, the special papers to fill out and read, the solemn entrance into the building through an officiated person (usually a security guard), the absolute understanding that we were to be on our most cordial behavior, and the unspoken acknowledgment among all present that we worshiped the same god, American citizenship—these were our practices. The ceremonious actions were penance for the sins we committed for being illegal as well as a show of reverence for the country we so longed to become permanent citizens of.

American "common sense" (Apple 1993) tells us that being undocumented is a euphemism for being illegal, illegitimate, inhuman. I grew up with a deeply ingrained reverence for the value of papeles—almost a sixth sense, or *facultad,*

> the capacity to see in the surface phenomena the meaning of deeper realities, to see the deep structure below the surface. It is an instant "sensing," a quick perception arrived at without conscious reasoning. It is an acute awareness mediated by the part of the psyche that does not speak, that communicates in images and symbols which are the faces of feelings, that is, behind which feelings reside/hide. (Anzaldúa 1987, p. 60)

My facultad originated in my intense desire to protect my family from the perils of undocumented status via a green card and then naturalization papers and became a growing concomitant urgency to acquire and produce as much documentation as possible in academic settings, with the similar hope of indemnity.

Here, I hope to tell my counter-story and to detail the direct connection between not having papeles in a US federal immigration context and the acquisition of inordinate amounts of papeles in a socioacademic context. Utilizing Apple's (1993) notion of *common sense* and Solórzano and Yosso's (2002) notion of *counter-storytelling*, I will chronicle the pivotal rite-of-passage experiences that took me from undocumented—an alien (non-citizen) who entered the United States without government authorization—to hyperdocumented: a person who produces exceeding amounts of documents, texts, and papers. Apple (1993) argues that

> the conventional approach to understanding how ideology operates assumes by and large that the ideology is "inscribed in" people simply because they are in a particular class position. The power of dominant ideas is either a given in which dominance is guaranteed, or the differences in "inscribed"

class cultures and ideologies will generate significant class conflict. In either case, ideology is seen as something that somehow makes its effects felt on people in the economy, in politics, in culture and education, and in the home, without too much effort. It is simply *there*. The common sense of people becomes common-sense "naturally" as they go about their daily lives, lives that are prestructured by their class position. (p. 15)

Solórzano and Yosso (2002) define counter-storytelling as a method of telling the stories of those people whose experiences are not often told (i.e., those on the margins of society). The counter-story is also a tool for exposing, analyzing, and challenging the master narrative of racial privilege. Counter-stories can shatter complacency, challenge the dominant discourse on race, and further the struggle for racial reform (p. 32).

This chapter's counter-stories problematize the notion of a central source of knowledge and being by providing a context to challenge "majoritarian stories," the kind of stories that, for example, "remind us that people who may not have the legal documents to 'belong' in the United States may be identified by their skin color, hair texture, eye shape, accent, and/or surname" (Solórzano and Yosso 2002, p. 29).

I employ these definitions of common sense and counter-storytelling to highlight the realities of a specific group of marginalized people by presenting alternatives beyond mainstream narratives (Solórzano and Yosso 2002) and demonstrating that they are not alone in their experiences. My use of a critical race methodology provides a space to engage alternative, real accounts that are counter to deficit-based stories of undocumented people. I hope to follow in the spirit of Anzaldúa's (1987) vision, where "we are articulating new positions in the 'in-between'" (pp. xxv–xxvi) that cross boundaries and integrate elements of narrative and theory, intersecting social identities as a seamless feature of text development. These counter-stories, then, become sources of strength, not weakness. Indeed, they are tools of survival and liberation (Delgado 1989).

My counter-story challenges the commonsense or perceived wisdom that undocumented immigrants are uneducated, powerless, and ignorant. It also opens a window on to the day-to-day realities of living with undocumented status and the ways in which these experiences can be leveraged in an agentic fashion. Undocumented immigrants are not alone in resisting the "standard formulae" (Solórzano and Yosso 2002, p. 29), which promote a view of a culturally deficient, legally defiant, and educationally disadvantaged group. They can arguably position themselves to acquire documents that call into question these standard stereotypical representations imposed on them by American common sense. By building a portfolio of documents to literally and figuratively demonstrate my worthiness and non-threatening disposition as a legal, legitimate human being, I show how I actively build my case to prove, beyond a reasonable doubt, the intactness of my humanity, intelligence, and resilience.

The seeming necessity and yearning for this recognition begs the questions,

> *Why, after gaining citizenship, do I continue to appeal for legitimacy, imagined or real?* and, *Has hyperdocumentation paid off for me personally, professionally, and for my family?* I argue that hyperdocumentation is one of the few ways to achieve a tangible, if not superficial, legitimacy as an undocumented immigrant within a national climate of fear and suspicion. However, I also question the worth and accompanying cost of hyperdocumentation and ask if it is perhaps an obsessive coping mechanism and potentially futile.

Perhaps my appeal for legitimacy is embodied in a belief that I need even more documentation to prove that I am indeed what I say I am or have earned what I say I have earned. This obsession began when, as a young child, I emigrated from Guatemala to the United States. My first memories of the importance of documentation came in the form of one of my childhood roles—translator. It was my job to accompany my mother to all of her activities (doctor's appointments, teacher conferences, grocery store, dentist, pediatrician, emergency room). Forms were second nature to me by the time I was seven years old. I knew the routine all too well and began to develop a nuanced skill for translating not only words but emotions and inferences. My handwriting improved with each "last name, first name, address" box I filled out. My writing speed increased, and I was always eager to get to the part where all my mom had to do was sign her name. These acts made me feel powerful and inculcated in me a sense of ownership of my family's "official" dealings. In a sense, I officiated all of the mundane, yet necessary, rites for everyday survival. Without me, I thought, how would those papers ever get filled out?

At the INS, I was similarly charged with pulling the numbered ticket from the magical red wheel that granted status by way of your proper place in line. I held that ticket for dear life; its presentation was required to verify the order of things. While the INS forms were available in Spanish, my parents still relied on me to confirm the accuracy of the information. Often I felt the remnants of the anxiety-produced stomach-ache that I had the nights before our INS visits, which found me in the bathroom either vomiting or with diarrhea. I debated in my mind whether or not to wake up my mother in the middle of those nights to let her know of my disease, but I would most often err on the side of allowing her more sleep. She, too, suffered physical ailments prior to our visits, mainly migraine headaches that she treated by tying a bandana tightly across her head and taking what remained of her recent prescription of Tylenol or Valium. This scenario repeated itself as our attempts at citizenship continued to be postponed with each visit. It was always a letdown, like the piercing of a balloon—all of the air we held inside us quickly dissipated, and we fell, ruptured, until the next inflation of dreams.

While my family resided in this space of dreams, we simultaneously lived in what Rosaldo (1998) calls a "racial nightmare of the imagination" (p. 86) in the space of American common sense. In many ways, "the undocumented speak with a measure of irony. They simultaneously accede to and resist their cultural homogenization. Even as they move toward co-optation, they prove unassimilable" (Rosaldo 1998, p. 84). In the rites of passage toward hyperdocumentation, there exists both a strong push toward wanting to be a part of American culture and a pull against losing one's native culture.

> If a social hierarchy's top and bottom appear to be zones of "zero degree" culture, so too is the zone of immigration, or the site where individuals move between two national spaces. Ideally, that is, from the dominant society's point of view, immigrants are stripped of their former cultures, enabling them to become American citizens, transparent, just like you and me, "people without culture." In ethnographic terms, so-called acculturation is probably better described as deculturation, or the production of postcultural citizens. (Rosaldo 1998, p. 81)

How does one acculturate without deculturating—or, *can* one acculturate without deculturating? How does the accumulation of documents drive one toward acculturation or deculturation? Rosaldo (1998) states that "the complex case of the undocumented suggests the need for a notion of the border conceived as a zone between stable places" (p. 85). And yet, at either end of the spectrum, whether those locations are stable becomes questionable. As Villenas (1996) explains in reference to her position as the colonizer/colonized Chicana ethnographer, "My space is a fluid space of crossing borders and, as such, a contradictory one of collusion and oppositionality, complicity and sub-version" (p. 729). Similarly, my attempt to acquire documents both isolated me from my native cultural norms and practices and caused me to keep them hidden by requiring me to put forward an aura of diminutive racelessness, which further facilitated my cultivation of American citizenship. I did not engage in an intentional tug of war; it was simply an insidiously acquired common sense, one that was fostered and developed in the daily practice of schooling.

This common sense was fed by the cultural artifacts of schooling—the golden star stickers for a "job well done" on a homework assignment, a certificate of perfect attendance awarded at the end-of-year assembly, a place in the statewide spelling bee, testing into the gifted and talented program, an invitation to be the emcee at the school Christmas pageant, and a reverence for the straight A report card. Every gesture—visual and behavioral—at school indicated high admiration for individual intelligence. The message was "Do good in school, do good in life." In this way, American common sense permeated the structures of school, dictating a strong sense of meritocracy that told me that "naturally," if I just studied hard enough, earned straight As, and worked diligently, I would achieve the American Dream.

Yet, below the surface of this common sense, I had an intuitive perception—a physical feeling—that there was something more to this mythology. I sensed an urgency to achieve academically that would never abate. In fact, this compelling need to succeed scholastically would serve as my quick and always ready defense mechanism against those who might question my American worthiness.

RITES OF PASSAGE

There is a story that we often tell in my family. In the center of my small childhood home of Richmond, California, stands a narrow hallway closet. Although the closet was meant to hold linens, with a family of eight, my parents chose to use it as a storage place for anything but what it was intended for. To me, it was a shrine, which I crammed with the achievement awards, report cards, dioramas, essays, and projects that I enthusiastically brought home from school. As adults, my older sister and I attempted to clean out that very closet and were tickled to find our elementary school diaries, secretly scribed with our deepest thoughts. The front flap of my sister's diary was decorated with a plethora of smiley faces.

Mine was filled with uninterrupted rows of perfectly aligned A+s. From an early age, I understood that documenting my academic achievement was prized. What I produced in school, and how teachers perceived and assessed my abilities, was the most powerful weapon I had against the odds that my family faced. In the life spaces between INS visits and daily errands, my facultad manifested itself in school, my haven.

Two events represent my urgent mission to hyperdocument in that they illustrate the gravity I placed on procuring officially documented accolades. In the sixth grade, I entered my first writing contest. The charge of the competition was to address the following topic: "Why we should honor our flag." Later, in the tenth grade, I was nominated and competed for Girls' State.[2] Both rites of passage illustrate my counter-story to the commonsense notions of illegal immigration.

Mrs. Garrigan, my sixth-grade teacher, introduced the essay contest with an announcement that ended "and whoever wins this will receive a $50 savings bond." Easy enough, I thought to myself. I can write about why we should honor our flag even though the US flag wasn't really my flag or something I could lay claim to. True to form, I jumped on the opportunity to receive another academic accolade, to acquire yet another document: a savings bond. I holed up at the El Sobrante Public Library in my usual corner spot, underneath Teen Fiction and next to the Reference section. I looked up all the materials I could possibly find on the American flag and created a barracks of books around me, notepad and pen in hand. What better way to manifest my entitlement to American citizenship than by winning a writing contest that addressed my patriotism? My entry was entitled "Why We Should Honor Our Flag, by Aurora Chang." I was selected as a finalist for the essay competition.

In retrospect, it seems wholly ironic that I felt so enthusiastic about this overt flag-waving act, and yet I was only imitating what I saw at home. My father—a true Republican's dream, a Latino immigrant with ultraconservative values—was the most loyal un-American American. Tears would well in his eyes at the sound of the American national anthem. Every Memorial Day and Fourth of July, he would fly the American flag, proudly hoisted on the side of our home for everyone to see. When we were kids, he took us on a family vacation to Reno, where we saw a show called "The Wild, Wild West," which, as all the advertisements suggested, had a patriotic theme. Everything was in red, white, and blue—including the blue, sequined thongs and red sparkly tassels the female performers wore. While my mother was furious with my father for exposing us kids to this adult show, my father was unfazed, his eyes again tearing up to "My country 'tis of thee, sweet land of liberty, of thee I sing." Little did he know that I, too, became emotional at the thought of achieving Americanness.

Then, when I was in tenth grade, in my ongoing quest to become the all-American girl, and completely in line with my academically competitive nature, I applied to a prestigious leadership program called Girls' State. Described as "a nonpartisan program that teaches young women responsible citizenship and love for God and country," Girls' State accepted only the cream of the crop, and, where I attended high school, the chosen girl held great prestige. The selection process consisted of a written application accompanied by a series of rigorous interviews requiring all sorts of knowledge of social capital: what to wear during a face-to-face interview, how to present oneself during these specific interactions, the post-interview courtesies, and all of the ways to exude a non-threatening yet confident, non-arrogant yet intelligent, non-masculine yet self-actualized, non-defiant yet curious, non-obnoxious yet witty, non-righteous yet principled demeanor. I had the privilege of acquiring some of these intangible skills throughout my academic schooling and socialization. At the end of the process, I received news that I had been chosen as the Girls' State representative from my school. My family and I celebrated over the weekend with *tamales, frijoles negros,* and *platanos fritos.*

But this celebration proved premature when, the following Monday, my principal called me into his office to regretfully inform me that because I was a non-citizen, I did not qualify for participation in Girls' State. I was denied the opportunity to exercise "responsible citizenship and love for God and Country" even though I had seemingly met all the requirements to effectively do so. My immigration status was the mortal sin that would not be forgiven. No matter the penance—be it a few more hours absorbing pages at the library, writing one more stellar essay, obtaining another certificate of merit, or receiving another impeccable report card—my lack of real papeles seemed to represent the ultimate evil. I dreamed of the moment when I could achieve, academically or otherwise, without the fear of having it all pulled out from under me. *When would I be saved?*

Redemption came on our day of naturalization. President Ronald Reagan's 1986 sweeping Immigration Reform and Control Act made any immigrant who had entered the country before 1982 eligible for amnesty— a word not usually associated with the father of modern conservatism. The law granted amnesty to nearly three million undocumented immigrants. My family and I were direct beneficiaries of amnesty. After being sworn in and officially naturalized, I ordered my first-ever lobster at A Sabella's, an Italian restaurant in San Francisco's Fisherman's Wharf. I had never seen my father so happy. I was quite certain that we had reached a milestone, and I naively concluded that any suffering associated with undocumented status had come to an absolute end. With naturalization papers in my hands, I was one with the American people. I was an American citizen.

And so it was time for me to finally relinquish my intense preoccupation with proving my academic merit. I would attend college and breeze through the luxurious realities of intellectual life. After all, what could be more indulgent than a circadian existence of learning, reading, and writing? But I quickly learned that although I was officially naturalized, the victory of this redemptive ceremony was short-lived. While naturalization legally endowed me with rights that were once not mine, I still lived within the same skin and female body, expressed myself with the same ethnic facial features, communicated with the same linguistic proclivities, and carried myself with the same protective (some would say defensive) facultad that my prior experiences had honed. In other words, despite my new-found de jure immigration status, I still faced the de facto actualities of being a once-undocumented, non-native-speaking brown woman. I was documented, but I was still unprotected from the consequential effects of intolerance. Now, more than ever, I understood that hyperdocumentation was critical to my survival, legal or not. I continued to accumulate my documents in the form of degrees, theses, awards, and the like in order to further build my case. I wanted people to know that I was qualified and deserving of my place in this country. In my mind, such documents would deem my qualifications—and me—unimpeachable.

Twenty years later and, seemingly, wiser, and with a cadre of degrees from the University of California, Berkeley, Stanford, and the University of Texas at Austin, I felt that these documents were significant moments in my academic trajectory. With each academic degree, I hoped to have added yet another layer of protection against racism, sexism, xenophobia. And on completing my dissertation, I once again felt as if I had reached a certain life milestone. As I walked across the stage to be hooded for my doctoral degree, I was literally fitted out in academic armor—a gown of velvet and wool, an ornate cap, and a series of embellishments. I wondered what it would be like to don my regalia on a daily basis—perhaps then my appearance would accurately represent who I thought myself to be. (I harkened back to this notion when I was recently asked to participate as an immigration "expert" in a campus-wide diversity effort.) But in reality, this latest rite of passage demonstrated otherwise.

A PhD a Doctor Does Not Make

One hundred and twenty people were packed together into an auditorium at Valley View Tech College, located in a small Midwest town that was once the headquarters for the Ku Klux Klan (KKK). The audience was gathered for "America Unites on Immigration," a panel discussion and one of the many events during the school's Diversity Week—an attempt to bring awareness to and encourage dialogue on issues not commonly spoken about in public settings. I was one of four panelists invited to share my knowledge about and experiences with immigration. I decided to tell my counter-story as a once undocumented immigrant. Nothing could have prepared me for what followed. Brad Johnson (personal communication, November 4, 2010), the event moderator, had given me a mild warning prior to the event in his e-mail reminder.

> I suspect that the conversation will eventually lead to the subject of undocumented immigration in the U.S. today. This will be a great opportunity for the panel to address many issues from legality and ethics to economics. Helping the audience see modern immigration in a historical context is also one of my desired outcomes of the evening. Most importantly, while there may be emotions in the room that evening, we have the opportunity to model civil discourse and show that people can listen to each other, and learn something in the process.

Before the panel began, I engaged in my normal routine. I went from table to table to introduce myself and make small talk. This was not something I enjoyed, but it is a skill my professional, academic, and home training had fostered within me. The goal of this exercise was always to take the temperature of the audience, and, in situations where I was visibly the other (brown, female, highly educated), it allowed me to present myself in a less-threatening fashion. "I'm one of you./I just got off of a long day at work./I have a family waiting at home./The weather sure is cold outside!/What do you do here?/Are you a native of Wisconsin?" I was not able to make it very far. With so many people in the room, I made strategic choices: the lone Asian woman, one of the three African Americans in the audience, the older white man in military garb, all of those in suits (who I presumed to be administrators of the college), and a handful of middle-aged white folks (who made up about 85 percent of the audience). My strategy involved a careful balance of making those who might feel uncomfortable more at ease and identifying potential allies of color in a sea of

the event on the DREAM Act next Friday. Susan, my wife, and I are registered and will be attending. I also may be bringing some of my students as well. Again, thank you for all that you did to make the event on Tuesday a success. (Brad Johnson,[3] personal communication, November 11, 2010)

I understood that my contribution to the panel was valuable, but at what expense? The fact that I was asked to tell my story for the benefit of others' learning (and/or pleasure in repudiating) was a double-edged sword. The telling of my counter-story was at once freeing, in that a space was provided to share my experiences, and exploitive, in that such a space was unsafe. In the e-mail exchanges with Brad Johnson, I sensed his sincerity. Indeed, he valued my personal story and complimented me by noting that instructors and students alike continued to discuss my talk days after the event. At the same time, I could not sleep that night and had a series of anxiety attacks in the days that followed. It took me weeks to stop the daily recounting to friends, family, colleagues, and students about the traumatic side effects of having my life on display and up for discussion. Was my choice to share my story worth the personal pain? Will I do it again? Certainly, hiding out and staying silent would appear safer than revealing my story and, yet, it is precisely my willingness to be vulnerable that garners strength within me. As it turns out, my refuge from danger no longer lies in concealing but rather in revealing my narrative.

I am left contemplating the mad scramble and furious quest for the terminal educational document. Has documentation deluded me into thinking that I have somehow escaped the mundane when actually I have positioned myself, and been positioned, to till the fields of academia without appropriate compensation, respite, or acknowledgment? This positioning poignantly parallels my path to citizenship, when I fought hard to repay my debt of illegality with the hope and expectation that I could breathe more easily and gain acceptance as an American. In the effort to challenge my position as an undocumented immigrant, I, in fact, comply with the very ideas that are arguably the source of discriminatory teachings, practices, and institutions. I contradict myself. I hoard documents so as to hide my undocumented status and, in the process, highlight the significance of documentation itself. Through hyperdocumentation, I employ my facultad to confront the rage and intolerance of American commonsense beliefs about immigration.

UNCOMMON SENSE: FACULTAD

Growing up, the everyday cues that I received regarding my immigration status were deeply embedded in the commonsense, xenophobic notions of what it means to be legal in the United States. The ideology surrounding immigration status is powerful, far-reaching, and insidious.

American common sense communicates that there are some who are legal and others who are illegal. This demarcation emphasizes a duality that easily equates legality with goodness and civility and illegality with evil and deviance. Continually operating out of this oppressive notion of common sense is not an easy space to escape. Daily, we ingest texts and images that profess the meaning of American citizenship and what deviates from it. As Rosaldo (1998) notes, "Images of 'illegal aliens' have been manufactured for the consumption of North American readers who at once see themselves as culturally transparent and feel threatened by the differences of class and culture" (p. 81). The image of young brown men swimming across the Rio Grande with plastic garbage bags on their backs, newspaper articles claiming that illegal immigrants drain the economy, photos of thick concrete walls erected on artificial borders—these are among the manufactured consumer commodities that help define American common sense regarding immigration. While it is perhaps easier to believe that only non-recent immigrants blindly embrace this notion, it is also just as true, if not truer, that recent immigrants incorporate these powerful visuals into their own being.

Common sense rejects and is shaped by how we understand our social world. I argue that, for an undocumented person, hyperdocumentation operates as a survival mechanism that responds to what has become an American common sense. Hyperdocumentation generates a semivisible force field—however imagined and to whatever extent credible—that protects one from undocumented status. Hyperdocumentation can be used in an agentic way as a tool of resistance. In other words, the resilience and ability to respond to situations that appear threatening are grounded on the instant perception (facultad) of danger. The fear of getting caught without papers, the fear of my teacher thinking I am less than capable because of my immigration status, the fear of being deported, the fear of believing that what I hear about immigrants is true, the fear of writing the wrong tax identification number in place of a Social Security number, the fear that even with official legal status, I will always look illegal, the fear of never feeling legitimate—these are all fears that have to be responded to in a moment with a wit that keeps you simultaneously guarded, afloat, and approachable. As an undocumented immigrant, I have learned to adopt a certain politeness, deference, and caution. And there are certain pivotal experiences in my life that establish milestones where this facultad is employed in a clearly illustrative way. The way I employed my facultad was by acquiring as many papeles or documents as possible as a means to create a sanctuary from and an armor against the peril of undocumented status.

I thought documentation would protect me from American common-sense notions of illegal immigration status. Yet, as my facultad has strengthened and become increasingly precise, I have gained a particularly strong understanding that security and self-preservation are not as straightforward as the necessary paperwork. Survival and success require much more than acquiring text on paper. When attempting to prove my American worthiness, I now know that there is a certain nuance to reading others that requires a specifically tailored response to each situation and context—an intangible, immediate sensing resulting from a refined mastery of facultad. At some times, interactions call for the slightest mention of a prestigious degree; at others, a subtle reference to a scholarly source or a humorous account of a tale involving a certain level of literary proficiency is needed. Such responses are not planned; rather, they are unconscious mediators between the lingering urgency to compensate for my lack of documentation and the obsessive need to hyperdocument. In my attempt to both relieve the anxiety and satisfy the compulsion of never being a truly "legitimate" American, I tell myself that my arsenal of documents is complete. My case for worthiness is valid and the paper trail exhaustive—that is, until the next time my merit is challenged.

NOTES

1. INS (Immigration and Naturalization Services) ceased to exist on March 1, 2003 (1933–2003). Since then, its primary functions are now housed in what is known as the US Citizenship and Immigration Services (USCIS) as part of the Department of Homeland Security.
2. American Legion Auxiliary, http://www.boysandgirlsstate.org/girls.html.
3. The name is a pseudonym and permission was provided to use the e-mail.

REFERENCES

Anzaldúa, G. (1987). *Borderlands: La frontera*. San Francisco: Aunt Lute Books.
Apple, M. (1993). *Official knowledge: Democratic education in a conservative age*. New York: Routledge.
Chang, A. (2011). Undocumented to hyperdocumented: A jornada of protection, papers and PhD status. *Harvard Educational Review, 81*(3), 508–520.
Delgado, R. (1989). Storytelling for oppositionists and others: A plea for narrative. *Michigan Law Review, 87*(8), 2411–2441.
Ellsworth, E. (1989). Why doesn't this feel empowering: Working through the myths of critical pedagogy. *Harvard Educational Review, 59*, 297–324.
Rosaldo, R. (1998). Ideology, place, and people without culture. *Cultural Anthropology, 3*(1), 77–87.
Solórzano, D. G., & Yosso, T. J. (2002). Critical race methodology: Counter-storytelling as an analytic framework for education research. *Journal of Qualitative Inquiry, 8*(1), 23–44.
Villenas, S. (1996). The colonizer/colonized Chicana ethnographer: Identity, marginalization, and co-optation in the field. *Harvard Educational Review, 66*(4), 711–731.

CHAPTER 3

Privileged and Undocumented: Toward a Borderland Love Ethic

As I sit with Guadalupe, one of the undocumented participants in my study, I begin to feel a common dis-ease. It is as if I am outside of myself, looking into the interview process from a corner on the wall. There I am, the once undocumented Guatemalan immigrant now turned hyperdocumented (Chang 2011) professor at a private university that costs $40,000 a year to attend, sitting a few feet from the subject of my study—a brilliant activist and a master's student in Social Work from another public university in the area, articulately and generously sharing his story with me. We could easily switch places, be it not for the 1986 Immigration Reform and Control Act (IRCA), also known as amnesty, when I was naturalized. I am slightly distracted and trying mightily to stay focused. I begin to have an internal dialogue with myself. "Who am I to be interviewing Guadalupe? He could just as easily interview me. He'd probably be better at it. Maybe this is just a common manifestation of imposter's syndrome." I can't help but wonder what Guadalupe must be thinking about this dynamic but, in that moment of the interview, I haven't established the rapport to ask.

I begin to experience a strong sense of survivor's guilt, the condition that occurs when a person perceives herself to have done wrong by surviving a traumatic event when others did not. The traumatic event we share,

---

This article was originally published in 2015 and is reprinted with permission given by the publishers (Chang 2015).

© The Author(s) 2018
A. Chang, *The Struggles of Identity, Education,
and Agency in the Lives of Undocumented Students,*
https://doi.org/10.1007/978-3-319-64614-5_3

albeit completely dissimilar in its details, is our border crossing. At that moment, I don't see Guadalupe. Instead, I clearly see the larger injustice embedded in this interaction—the inhumane, nonsensical, and xenophobic policies around immigration that have somehow deemed me worthy of citizenship and Guadalupe in a limbo of DACAmentation. I heed Dowbor's words of warning (1997), that capitalism is the generator of scarcity. In a country with an abundance of all things material, the gap between the rich and poor grows each minute. Depending on what is politically and economically palatable to those in power, commodities like citizenship are strategically distributed. My citizenship was bought and sold in the political marketplace of the day. For Guadalupe, it simply is not for sale today. I am perplexed and angry because Guadalupe's situation is unfair and I can't understand where I fit into this power dynamic. Something within me feels culpable. What was once a shameful secret, my undocumented status, is now my ticket to access my study participants.

In this paper, I seek to explore the tensions of what it means to be a "deserving" native researcher. I begin by experimenting with the meaning of a *borderland love ethic* as a theoretical framework that centers on nurturing our strength to love in spaces of contention, tolerance of ambiguity as a revolutionary virtue, and humbly beginning anew again and again. Drawing from an extended interview with a participant (Guadalupe) of a larger study about undocumented students, I describe our positionalities with respect to privilege and undocumented status as the central foci. I use my own dilemma of understanding and reconciling my position as a once undocumented immigrant to a now hyperdocumented (Chang 2011) native researcher, studying undocumented people, to work through the possibility of a borderland love ethic. Relying on previous work on the dilemmas of native ethnography, I explore the specific struggle of being undocumented (native) and privileged (non-native) by comparing and contrasting my experience as researcher and Guadalupe's experience as research participant. I offer a borderland love ethic as an "untested feasibility" (Darder 2003, p. 502) for approaching our work in a way that sustains both researcher and participant and stays true to our integrity. Relying primarily on the theoretical works of Anzaldúa (1987), Darder (2003), and hooks (2000), I ask how we as scholars enact love in our research amidst our seemingly contradictory positions of oppression and privilege. I contend that one possibility is by employing a borderland love ethic that embraces ambiguity, rejects binary positions, and humbly acknowledges our constant state of arriving, both as researchers and participants. A borderland love ethic allows researchers to engage with research participants in a conversation among equally broken subjects. That is, the researcher is a subject of academia, at once studying and being studied, while the participant is a subject of research, at once researching and being researched. In fact, a borderland love ethic feeds this cycle of "re-searching" our own subjectivities, searching again and again, infinitely, as we move dynamically and amorphously within, between, and outside of academic borders.

LOVE AND RESEARCH

It may seem counterintuitive to conceive of love in the context of research. This is because we are taught that research is unemotional, distant, and objective, rather than centering the self and Others as sentient, complex, and intersectional beings. "Though epistemologically and methodologically indefensible, this view is still largely dominant in social science practice" (Greenwood and Levin 1998, p. 53), and while this positivistic credo is prevalent, it is in direct opposition to the kind of research practices that are grounded in love because it removes humanity from the scientific process and, in its absence, is replaced by a mythological objectivity. Love, in the context of educational research, feels awkward because, as bell hooks (2000) understands, we are perplexed about how to talk about love, hold conflicting beliefs of what love entails, and/or perpetuate overly romanticized myths about the meaning of love. This is especially true as love relates to education. This is how Antonia Darder (2003) articulates love:

> I am neither speaking of a liberal, romanticized, or merely feel-good notion of love that so often is mistakenly attributed to this term nor the long-suffering and self-effacing variety associated with traditional religious formation. Nothing could be further from the truth. If there was anything that Freire consistently sought to defend, it was the freshness, spontaneity, and the presence embodied in what he called an "armed love—the fighting love of those convinced of the right and the duty to fight, to denounce, and to announce." (Freire 1998, pp. 42, 497)

For me, love has always been inextricably bound with education because I have always connected love to struggle, conviction, and voice. My roots as an undocumented immigrant from Guatemala exposed me to the type of tragedy, loss, and corruption that could only be understood and combatted with a spirit of armed love. As Darder (2003) so articulately notes, love is not about butterflies and roses: "Instead, it is a love that I experienced as unconstructed, rooted in a committed willingness to struggle persistently with purpose in our life and to intimately connect that purpose with what [Freire] called our 'true vocation' – to be human" (p. 498).

A BORDERLAND LOVE ETHIC

The theoretical framework I propose, a borderland love ethic, is a hybrid of three concepts: borderland theory, a love ethic, and interactionality. Specifically, a borderland love ethic encompasses: (1) Anzaldúa's notion of borderlands and the mestiza consciousness required to claim all parts of one's identity within a provisional space constructed with one's own feminist architecture (Anzaldúa 1987); (2) hooks' (2000) and Darder's (2003) reconceptualization of love as an "armed" love that is global in its vision, intimately engaged with the collective good, and oriented toward the continual process of self-actualization; and (3) Chavez' (2013) notion of interactionality that builds on the critical concept of intersectionality (Crenshaw 1991) as "a form of rhetorical confrontation that begins critique from the roots of a problem or crisis and methodically reveals how systems of power and oppression interact with one another in ways that produces subjects, institutions, and ideologies and that enable and constrain political response" (p. 51). I suggest that a borderland love ethic melds Anzaldúa's (1987) definition of borderland and hooks' (2000) definition of a love ethic that leads to agentic action propelled by interactionality (Chavez 2013). Anzaldúa (1987) says:

> Borders are set up to define the places that are safe and unsafe, to distinguish *us* from *them*. A border is a dividing line, a narrow strip along a steep edge. A borderland is a vague and undetermined place created by the emotional residue of an unnatural boundary. (p. 25)

bell hooks (2000) defines a "love ethic" as "choosing to work with individuals we admire and respect; by committing to give our all to relationships; by embracing a global vision wherein we see our lives and our fate as intimately connected to those of everyone else on the planet" (p. 88), "a belief that honesty, openness, and personal integrity need to be expressed in public and private decisions" (p. 88) and "concern for the collective good of our nation, city, or neighbor" (p. 98). It incorporates the kind of *convivencia* (Coll 2004) that is had by "getting to know one another by spending time, talking, and doing things together, as well as learning more about their shared collective concerns and experiences" (p. 189). Interactionality (Chavez 2013) highlights the complicated and dynamic way in which our intersectional identities, power and systems of oppression intermesh, interlock, intersect, and interact. In this way, "it holds in tension both the predictable ways oppression and power manifest in relation to and upon particular bodies while also carrying possibilities for creative and complicated responses to oppression" (p. 58).

A borderland love ethic, then, is an ethic that can be understood as, at once, undetermined and specific to each individual, resulting from the emotional residue of an unnatural boundary as manifested by varying dichotomies. A borderland love ethic encourages us to make purposive public and private choices as researchers about how much we give, to whom we give, and why we give, all in a quest for an interconnected collective good with a clear understanding that rejects essentialist compartmentalization of identities and embraces the inherent tensions involved in the power dynamics of conducting research. A borderland love ethic must engage three tenets: (1) nurturing our space to love in spaces of contention, (2) tolerance of ambiguity as a revolutionary virtue, and (3) humbly beginning anew, again and again.

NURTURING OUR STRENGTH TO LOVE IN SPACES OF CONTENTION

As researchers with multiple identities, we are inevitably bound in spaces of contention. Our identities can be in conflict with one another or with those of others. Our work is contentious because it is not in isolation; rather, it is inextricably connected to the worlds around us. This contentiousness takes a toll on our health (Gutiérrez y Muhs et al. 2012) if we fail to nurture the necessary strength to remain centered and exercise love in our practice. hooks (1994), in her discussion of engaged pedagogy, states that holistic education emphasizes well-being:

> That means that teachers must be actively committed to a process of self-actualization that promotes their own well being if they are to teach in a manner that empowers students.

Thich Nhat Hanh emphasized that the "practice of a healer, therapist, teacher or any helping professional should be directed toward his or herself first, because if the helper is unhappy, he or she cannot help many people" (p. 15).

What if we were to translate this engaged pedagogy into an engaged research practice where the research actively commits to a process of self-actualization, where she directs her own practices toward herself first and in this way models for and empowers participants in this process? As a once undocumented immigrant, I must acknowledge my privilege as a current US citizen and active member in the same institutions that oppress those undocumented people that I claim to advocate for and write about. Yes, I love working with undocumented people but at times I feel emotionally spent because I am not taking the time to acknowledge the sacredness of my own intactness. What good am I in a situation where I don't have the energy or disposition to truly be present in listening to their stories? Audre Lorde proclaimed, "Caring for myself is not self-indulgence, it is self-preservation, and that is an act of political warfare." Likewise, caring for ourselves, refusing to give in to dominant narratives of unworthiness and undeservingness as researchers, especially as marginalized researchers, is absolutely necessary for self-preservation. It is a love ethic manifesto, screaming, I will not allow this process to dehumanize me, to damage me, to crush me. Furthermore, I would proffer that a borderland love ethic honors the emotional well-being of undocumented students themselves involved in navigating love, in all its iterations, across borders (Abrego 2014). Dr. Martin Luther King Jr. said, "We're split up and divided against ourselves. And there is something of a civil war going on within all of our lives. There is a recalcitrant South of our soul revolting against the North of our soul. And there is this continual struggle within the very structure of every individual life" (*Loving Your Enemies*, Delivered at Dexter Avenue Baptist Church Montgomery, Alabama, November 17, 1957). We require a respite in warring with our multiple selves, a borderland space that allows for dynamic movement and repositioning.

TOLERANCE OF AMBIGUITY AS A REVOLUTIONARY VIRTUE

Anzaldúa (1987) spoke of the importance of our tolerance for ambiguity. She notes that for a mestiza: "In perceiving conflicting information and points of view, she is subjected to a swamping of her psychological borders. She has discovered that she can't hold concepts or ideas in rigid boundaries" (p. 101). A borderland love ethic embraces the intersectional, oppositional, and transgressive border identities that embody us. As Negrón-Gonzales (2014) notes through her work with migrant youth, "As their lives are fundamentally characterized by the legal and social contradiction that arises from growing up in the United States yet facing barriers to full participation in US society, the production of migrant youth illegality is a process marked by both distinct forms of regulation and exclusion as well as a sustained connection to institutions central to US society" (p. 275). As undocumented people, we embody ambiguous contradictions. We are implicated in our positions as academics. We are oppressed as faculty of marginalized backgrounds. We were once a part of an othered community. Now we are part of privileged communities as well. We have entered into new realms of otherness we knew not existed. Our very bodies and mouths silence the otherwise powerful and incite the roots of hatred. All at the same time and ever changing, our identities sway, ebb, shift and evolve. We, like those we study, are native and semi-native and non-native within our own communities. Rather than see this as a deficit, we need to consider adopting this ambiguity as a revolutionary virtue. It takes extraordinary courage to accept every part of who we are and engage every part of who we are in our research process. In the gathering of patience and quiet within a space of not knowing, we can sit with our contradictions and "operate in a pluralistic mode—nothing is thrust out, the good, the bad, and the ugly, nothing rejected, nothing abandoned. Not only does she sustain contradictions, she turns the ambivalence into something else" (Anzaldúa 1987, p. 101).

Humbly Beginning Anew Again and Again

These contradictions require us to constantly reconstruct our identities. Our research processes require us to engage with a new set of people, emotions, and identities. A borderland love ethic embraces the capacity to always begin anew, to make, to reconstruct, and to live in the split. Not only does it embrace intersectionality but further evolves this paradigm through a framework of radical interactionality:

> an idea that builds on the women of color feminist notion of intersectionality. It is a form of rhetorical confrontation that begins critique from the roots of a problem or crisis and methodically reveals how systems of power and oppression interact with one another in ways that produce subjects, institutions, and ideologies that enable and constrain political response. (Chavez 2013, p. 51)

Chavez (2013) elaborates on her term "interactionality" by stating that it "is equipped for addressing the complexity of a problem's roots" (p. 57) and "has been advanced to understand the complicated interworking of power that constitutes the situation of people who experience interlocking oppressions" (p. 57). Interactionality "works against reductionism and purity, promoting instead a perspective that accounts for differences that make a difference in how people can maneuver their worlds" (p. 58). We operate interactionally, under consistent change and are naïve to resist this state of always arriving embodied in our interactional selves. As Freire (1993) declares: "Refuse to bureaucratize the mind, to understand and to live as a process—live to become—is something that always accompanied me throughout life. This is an indispensable quality of a good teacher" (p. 98). I believe that as researchers, we too can benefit from honoring our process by understanding that our identities are never concretized; we are always in a state of renewal. When we engage with our participants, we start anew by explicitly sharing our vulnerability as works in progress, co-producers of knowledge and people with pain. Our research process can be one of renewal where we gather what we have learned from our previous experiences and then incorporate those lessons into our new practice. We will never be experts because knowledge is never static therefore our expertise is always obsolete. That's why we begin again, each time, knowing that we enter this work with a spirit of awareness, humility, and regeneration.

THE MOMENT

What follows is a moment during my interview with Guadalupe that prompted my reflection of the intersection of undocumented status and privilege. Following the advice of Abu-Lughod (1991), I "focus[ed] closely on [a] particular individual and [his] changing relationships" in an effort to "necessarily subvert the most problematic connotations of culture: homogeneity, coherence and timelessness" (p. 476). In other words, Guadalupe does not necessarily represent all undocumented students nor does our exchange represent all of my exchanges with all of my participants. Instead, this moment serves as a phenomenological window into discussing how a borderland love ethic might play into our research process. I thought I was alone in recognizing the national discursive disease around immigration advocate strategy and my aforementioned dis-ease as a researcher. Like a cancer, essentialized notions of depictions of undocumented immigrants can insidiously toxicize immigration reform discourses, creating a single story that privileges "deserving" immigrants as uniquely "DREAMers," as an example, at the expense of the other millions of immigrants that have not had the same academic opportunities, forms of capital, and/or luck. These singular notions feed my own dis-ease as a researcher, a form of epistemological discomfort, that emerges from my apparent undocumented experience's lack of politically expedient authenticity (that of poor, uneducated, brown immigrant crossing the desert or river, drawn to a better economic life in America). They also underscore the nature of my "nativeness" to the undocumented student lived experience. However, Guadalupe revealed that he too was grappling with his own struggle of duality around his position as a "privileged" undocumented student:

Interviewer: How do you feel about the DREAM Act and DACA?
Guadalupe: So I never liked the DREAM Act. I didn't apply for the DREAM Act. I don't know whether it was because it was just going to be me. It was not going to apply to our parents; they are still deportable. I mean they can get deported. So, I mean I don't like DACA because it assumes that people just came here and are doing things that are not the right way or whatever. It kind of goes with this idea of pull yourself by the bootstraps society that we live in. I mean what is going to happen with the rest of the immigrants here? We don't even talk about who has been deported from DACA.

Guadalupe spoke adamantly about the lack of fairness implicit in legislation like the DREAM Act and DACA, explaining, in so many words, that to apply for and receive such benefits equated to leaving others behind such as his parents, friends, and other students. He asserts that such legislation makes a lot of assumptions, particularly about the deservingness of a tiny minority of immigrants to obtain minimal rights while leaving millions of others to fend for themselves. Guadalupe honed in on the very minute sliver of the undocumented population that benefits from such legislation and those of us (he and I included) who luxuriate in academic conversations around DACA-related issues.

Unless you are an academic, there is no talk in the media of who has benefited from DACA; the poor haven't benefited because they can't afford the paperwork fee and most of them had to drop out of high school to help the parents. I think now it's even harder because of the ways that they are framing of DREAM Act. Sure if I am the valedictorian of Harvard University, of Stanford University or whatever, then I'm good. But it is hard to find those students; there are so few valedictorians. I mean there is going to be only one valedictorian in every school.

He situates himself as part of that minority and explains his perceived privilege as perpetuated by the assumptions others make of him.

Guadalupe: Yeah I mean so sometimes I feel like I hang out with two different crowds. Like more of my work crowd which seems to be kind of Whiter and young people ... most of them are older. But there, you have some kind of privilege; there are certain expectations of you being a typical Latino. And then my fellow students wonder... my classmates that I went with to high school that always see me as the guy who is going to do good things. My dad had a decent job, a stable job. I was a nerd in school so they always see me as the guy that is coming to do good things, the guy that is happy, the guy that has economic stability. But you don't know it, I mean they don't know beyond that. I think right now that I am in Midwest City University, there are a lot of assumptions when I tell them that I am an undocumented student, even to my friends.

Guadalupe describes the pressure he feels as an undocumented Latino with academic, social, and economic privilege to live up to certain expectations and to carry himself as one who is happy, successful, and, ultimately, a good guy with few problems. Guadalupe's conflicted identity as both oppressed and privileged does not fit neatly into a compartment. His identity resides in a borderland, a location that is in direct opposition to the essentialist depictions of the undocumented Latino. A borderland love ethic moves away from this tension to one of embracing and nurturing our ability to love in this space of seeming contention. Rather than viewing Guadalupe's borderland identity as a space of angst, it can be refashioned as a revolutionary virtue that is at peace within its ambiguity. It resists the need to hide aspects of our identity that seem incongruent and instead invites us to boldly and humbly announce its complexity as an agentic tool of resistance.

One, you have money, you are nerd, you are happy, your life is solely happy and I mean that's not necessarily true. Like I work hard. I am happy but I mean there are some days that I'm happy, there are some days that I am not happy. But there are just a lot of assumptions. Mainly I don't even tell my friends that I go to Midwest City University or that I have this job. Every once in a while, I complain about my job to someone and they are like, what are you complaining about? That shit happens to me every day, friends that are working in restaurants, friends that are working in different places. For them, my complaints are their day to day life. I don't even go there....

Everyday talk such as complaining about work become sources of contention for Guadalupe, as, relative to his friends who are do manual labor and/or operate under abusive work conditions, he is in a place of privilege through his office job. Even his upbringing, where his father, albeit undocumented, made a decent living; his academic achievement; and his general upbeat disposition situate him uncomfortably as one who simultaneously struggles through being undocumented and has the luxury of having the financial means and academic capital to access what is deemed as success.

Through Guadalupe's discussion of his own perceived privilege, I was prompted to further think about my own complex identity as researcher relative to my participants. In him, I saw a reflection of myself. He was beating himself up, questioning his right to complain, feeling guilty about what he does have and can use to help others. He withdraws. He "doesn't go there." He puts on a happy face. How often have I reacted the exact same way in response to my study participants, disconnecting from my genuine feelings? And what does this say about my research process? How can we, as undocumented people at different ends of the immigration status spectrum, be kinder to ourselves and, in this way, refuse to reproduce the kind of blaming and shaming already imposed upon us by the master narrative of undocumented immigrants as undeserving, criminal, and inhumane?

GUADALUPE'S BORDER CROSSING

Here, I relay a bit about Guadalupe's border-crossing experience, followed by my own, as an exercise in contrasting knowledges of what it means to *ir al Norte*. I contrast our border-crossing experiences to highlight the heterogeneity of undocumented experiences and simultaneously expose the commonality we share in our framing of feelings about and struggles with this so-called position of occupying spaces of both privilege and undocumented status. I chose Guadalupe as one participant to situate my analysis of my positionality as a native undocumented researcher, emphasizing the particularity of our conversations rather than generalizing. Guadalupe is a 30-year-old Mexican immigrant who came to this country when he was 11 years old. He crossed through Tijuana, Mexico.

> At the age of 11, my grandpa, my dad, decided we all needed to be in one place instead of everywhere but this time I had a brother, two brothers and a sister so we made the journey to the United States. I didn't really want to leave, my first attempt to cross the border kind of ended sadly. I was deported. We were trying to cross with this 65-year-old man through Ciudad Juarez. My grandparents had left us in Juarez so they didn't know where we were. So, we crossed my brother and me he was 8 or 9. I was 11. To add to it, we were going to tell the agencies that we were going to the mall that was on the Ciudad Juarez side. But that didn't work out. So, we were taken to the equivalent of the department of child and welfare services in the United States; that is what it is called in Mexico. So my grandparents didn't know where we were; they looked everywhere for 2 ½ days to see where they can find us. So finally they found us. We were back but I think for the two days I didn't want to eat; the only thing I wanted to do was cry.
>
> So, we went back to the Tijuana, we have family members in Tijuana and about two weeks later I was ready to go back but my younger brother and my sister were already in the U.S. They crossed the first time so now it was just me and my mom who also got deported, detained because of the time we were in Tijuana but my sister and my brother were already on this side. So, there was a question whether do they go back, how do we do this? Should we come here? So, I was the last one to enter the country and I mean I didn't want to come, I just wanted to leave. I remember the perception in my town especially from my teacher was kind of bad perception of El Norte; you are going to El Norte which is kind of bad. The imperialist, capitalist place; this is what my teacher would tell us; she was a very revolutionary teacher. Besides, in my third and fifth grade I had the same teacher and she just had a bad perception about it.

Guadalupe's story is not one of eager departure to escape poverty, seeking opportunity in the land of milk and honey. As he so vividly recalls, going to El Norte was not something that his community members reveled. Quite the opposite, this traversing of the border was more of a paradigmatic shift, leaving one's home culture and stepping foot into the disturbing land of imperialism and capitalism. There is a common myth that immigrants come to the United States looking forward, but, as we well know as immigrants, we may be walking forward but our heads are always looking back. Guadalupe, not unlike many immigrants, came to the United States with the intention of temporarily resettling but always with the hope of going back to their native country. It is less of an American Dream we seek and more of an American daydream we long for that we will one day snap out of only to return to our national reality.

My border crossing resulted from different circumstances yet, again, not for the reasons that the dominant narrative would have us believe; we did not seek a land of opportunity. In fact, we were destined to lose our once upper-middle-class socioeconomic status by leaving our native Guatemala. Amidst the multiple and multi-terrained borders that Guadalupe and I crossed—geographically, academically, and personally—I theorize about the ways in which we might embrace these topographies.

RESEARCHER'S CROSSING OF MULTIPLE BORDERS

Geographical Border

When I was five years old, my papa fled to the United States, unbeknownst to my pregnant mama and my then sister and brother (we would grow to a family of eight). It was Good Friday, 1979, 36 years ago to the day. Eventually, my mama, being who she is, found my papa and we landed in West Covina, California (I have skipped over a mirage of important details but as with most immigrant stories, there are secrets I will not share, *cosas que no se dicen*). My parents were the first in their families to attend college. My papa had his master's degree in civil engineering; my mama had some years of college under her belt—this socioeconomic status allowed us to get a visa through Guatemalan consulate connections. In a Guatemalan context, we were financially well off. As we know, class is something that rarely rears its head in the context of the immigrant narrative since media images would have us believe that all immigrants share a monolithic experience that begins with crossing the border by desert or river. However, the less told story (probably because it doesn't incite xenophobic sentiments therefore serving no political purpose) is that many undocumented immigrants go to *El Norte* by obtaining a temporary visa, flying on a plane, and overstaying their time limit. This was my family's case.

Academic Border

Fast-forward to my life as a tenure-track assistant professor engaged in research about currently undocumented people. I am no longer undocumented, benefiting, through no effort of my own, from all the rights and privileges associated with American citizenship. I sit at my desk, overlooking Lake Michigan, reviewing interview transcripts, coding data, reading books of theory, and slowly in time recognizing only a blurring of the life I once occupied. The 37th floor at Lakeshore East is far away from the realities of my family's once undocumented life. The distance—geographical, spatial, and emotional—renders me floating in a space that is "betwixt and between," as Anzaldúa might say. I am certainly not the first nor will I be the last to reside in the borderland of research and researched, native and non-native, oppressed and oppressor.

Personal Border

In the same vein that Guadalupe questions his position and deservingness as an undocumented person with privilege, I question my own deservingness of this role as researcher, given my once undocumented status, and work to chart my path toward a *borderland love ethic* as a native researcher (Villenas 1996), to understand and reconcile my position as a once undocumented immigrant to a now hyperdocumented (Chang 2011) researcher studying undocumented people. I want to explore the ways in which love of self and love of the Other play out in my research process. As Abu-Lughod (1991) explains, "because of their split selves, feminist and halfie anthropologists travel uneasily between speaking 'for' and speaking 'from'" (p. 470). Similarly, I speak in the borderland tongue *from* being once undocumented and *for* those who are currently undocumented. I own the tensions I experience around "deservingness" and representation as a native undocumented researcher. I find it necessary to unpack my positionality as it relates to my current work with undocumented students and specifically, in relationship to Guadalupe, one of my undocumented student participants who led me to problematize my position an insider (native) researcher. My once undocumented status feels null and void amidst those who currently live their undocumented status.

THE INSIDER (NATIVE)/OUTSIDER DILEMMA

Many scholars have problematized the insider/outsider dilemma. Arguments regarding this dilemma have ranged from lack of objectivity, an insider's knowledge not being sufficient, to questioning the extent of a native anthropologist's nativeness, to enacting colonizer and colonized practices. Abu-Lughod (1991) explained that "the problem with studying one's own society is alleged to be the problem of gaining enough distance" and continues on, "these worries suggest that the anthropologist is still defined as a being who must stand apart from the Other, even when he or she seeks explicitly to bridge the gap" (p. 468). Narayan (1993) asked, "How native is a native anthropologist?" In her discussion of native anthropology, she problematizes the value given to so-called native anthropologists and the dichotomous nature of the native (insider) versus regular (outsider) researcher, arguing for enactment of hybridity in our texts where researchers are "viewed in terms of shifting identifications amid a field of interpenetrating communities and power relations" (p. 671). After all, she insists, who is this generic subject, "the native"? Instead, she focuses on the importance of seeing our participants as people with voices, views, and dilemmas rather than as an essentialized Other. She claims that by situating ourselves as subjects simultaneously touched by life experiences and swayed by professional concerns, we can acknowledge the hybrid and positioned nature of our identities.

Sofia Villenas (1996) asked, "What happens when members of low-status and marginalized groups become university-sanctioned 'native' ethnographers of their own communities" (p. 712)? She argues that while qualitative researchers theorize their own privilege in relation to their research participants, native researchers must deal with their own marginalizing experiences in relation to dominant society. The native researcher becomes both the colonizer, via her position as university expert investigator, and the colonized, as a member of the othered community she studies. She finds herself complicit in the manipulation of her own identities and participating in her own colonization and marginalization. She challenges majority culture researchers to call upon their own marginalizing experiences and find a space for the emergence of new identities and discourse in the practice of solidarity with marginalized peoples.

Jacob (2006) discusses the ways in which power dynamics affect the knowledge production processes involved in research. She focuses on researcher reflexivity and the problematics and power dynamics involved when a native attempts to "go researcher." She finds how the complications of researcher subjectivity, research ethics, and identity work took shape during her research process. Chicana scholars Patricia Zavella (1996) and Maxine Baca Zinn (1979) explore racial subjectivities within their research, discussing the dilemmas that insiders face during the research process, such as abiding by community norms and writing in a way that accurately and respectfully represents the community while adhering to academic protocols. Because we present the Other as we present ourselves (Abu-Lughod 1991), native researchers "speak with a complex awareness and investment in reception ... forced to confront squarely the politics and ethics of their representations. There are no easy solutions to their dilemmas" (p. 469).

Many of these dilemmas lie in shifting/evolving identities of the researcher relative to the researched. For example, researchers, once part of a lower socioeconomic class, trouble their new positionality as upper-middle-class professors. Others who came from families with little formal education note the challenges with their newfound highly educated status. Still others discuss evolutions of their sexual, racial, and ethnic identities over time and the ways in which these identifications contrast with that of their participants who are from communities which they once identified with but no longer.

As a once undocumented immigrant conducting research on currently undocumented immigrants, I am met with similar conundrums of native researchers but specifically with one very poignant impasse. Immigration status is an entity that, while remaining with you as an aspect of your identity (regardless of immigration status), is something over which individuals have little to no personal control over. In other words, immigration status is not an identity that you can self-select; the state determines that identity. Therefore in engaging with my participants, I am, in fact, an institutional agent acting from the same place where others once limited my life's potentiality. I did not pull myself up from my bootstraps to arrive at this documented point—the state determined my status. And because the nature of migration and immigration policy is one that is always in flux, what applied then is not what applies now. The political environment, the laws and executive orders, the resources, and the global climate around immigration require a relevant, current, and thorough understanding in order to then disseminate appropriate, responsible information to those seeking a pathway to citizenship. When I conducted studies on another native community of mine, the multiracial community, I was able to envision possible scenarios down the road, commiserating with my participants and anticipating possible outcomes with regard to identity development and life choices. I don't have this vision with undocumented students because I, we, am at the disposition of lawmakers. Certainly, we can and have exerted agency in this regard, but there is a ceiling. There is a dangerous line I tread that balances hopefulness with the political and legal realities of this country. There are too many unknown variables in the lives of undocumented students to determine what may be ahead. So as a researcher who strives to be socially just, what is my role as I interact with my participants? In one of my researcher journal entries, I focused on the visceral discomfort, symptomatic of my duality.

> I am pulled. My body feels as if it will split in half if I continue to do this work. Every time I interview another undocumented student, I feel that I will come undone. I know this work is important. I feel a deep connection with my participants. I push hard through feelings of inferiority. It is like grieving. The once undocumented Guatemalan immigrant in me feels survivor guilt. The researcher in me feels the potential lack of ethics involved in the lack of reciprocal benefit. The teacher in me mourns for the wasted educational potential. The neighborhood girl in me is wading in a new adolescence where the more I learn, the less I know, the less I understand. The border lives and dies in me and through every interview I conduct, every word I transcribe, every memory that reemerges. And I have it easy, so easy. But this work of researching is not fate; it is a choice. This is not a feeling, this is an action. I am lost in love. (Research journal entry, 1/15/2015)

In another piece, I discuss in detail my journey from undocumented to hyperdocumented immigrant, perhaps perpetuating the now common belief that in order to qualify for US citizenship, not only do you have to follow all the rules and be behaviorally upstanding but also be a straight A student, activist, and community heroine. I often think of this notion that Guadalupe also raised in his interview, of "deserving immigrant," and ruminate on the psychological and emotional stakes that we are holding. How does my own research (including my choice of participants) feed this myth?

How do we so-called native researchers reconcile luxuriating in the powerful abstraction of the ivory tower while claiming a native stance in solidarity with our study participants? How do we negotiate dichotomous positions of oppression and privilege as we carry out our research, specifically in the context of studying people of undocumented status? Villenas' (1996) notion of the colonizer/colonized Chicana ethnographer:

> I am the colonized in relation to the greater society, to the institution of higher learning, and to the dominant majority culture in the research setting. I am the colonizer because I am the educated, "marginalized" researcher, recruited and sanctioned by privileged dominant institutions to write for and about Latino communities. (p. 714)

While undocumented people are dying crossing borders, their remains often unidentifiable from the scorch of the desert heat, mothers and children are detained at privately funded, grossly profitable detention centers (Heidbrink 2014) often called *hieleras* (iceboxes) because of the chilling air conditioning that remains on 24 hours a day; LGBTQ detainees suffering horrendous abuses after fleeing their home countries from persecution only to find worse treatment within disguised prison walls—I write. I want to believe that this is my activism. But to go from a once undocumented child, crossing the geographical southern border to a now hyperdocumented professor, crossing the metaphorical border is a leap that situates me in a unique borderland of sorts. Like Guadalupe, I grapple with the ways in which my privileged status interrupts, impacts, and colors my interactions. I believe we must be intentional in the ways in which we approach our research so that we leverage our multiple, often ambiguous identities as sources of strength, love, and humility. I offered an approach that might help to take us closer toward a borderland love ethic.

CONTRADICTIONS

A borderland love ethic is an attempt to reconcile a removed privileged identity with an identity in solidarity with research participants' struggles against oppression. My borderland identity as a now documented researcher is quite different than Guadalupe's identity as an undocumented graduate student of color. The act of writing about having once been undocumented creates an immediate riff between researcher and participant with the ironic twist that such an identity perhaps facilitated my entrée into the lives of my participants and initiated a type of familiar rapport. The truth of the matter is that I am able to enact a borderland ethic because of my privilege. Guadalupe, on the other hand, is always arriving. Even though he resides in the United States and is considered successful, he is still absent in many ways, living his social reality with the knowledge that legality remains an impossibility.

CONCLUSION

Often, researchers of marginalized statuses and identities privately wrestle with powerfully mixed emotions regarding their positionalities as researchers and the positionalities of those who they research. This can lead to debilitating feelings, including imposter syndrome, survivor's guilt, and analysis paralysis. This inquiry is important because it invites a conversation, one that is open, nonjudgmental, and courageous about the emotional and practical realities of a native researcher in academia. As hooks (2000) so beautifully notes:

> To live our lives based on the principles of a love ethic (showing care, respect, knowledge, integrity and the will to cooperate), we have to be courageous. Learning how to face our fears is one way we embrace love. Our fear may not go away, but it will not stand in the way. (p. 101)

The seemingly contradictory positions of privilege and solidarity with our study participants are important in understanding how we can purposively instill love in our research practice and perhaps become transformed in the process.

We have all heard the adage that love is a verb, not a noun, and this is particularly true in research. As researchers, we have been trained, for the most part, to see participants as the researched, the subjects, the nouns versus seeing them as living, dynamic, active verbs. This paradigmatic change transforms the research process from one of bystander, objective observer to engaged, subjective partaker. It allows us to "live and love in the present—as much personally as politically" (Darder 2003, p. 499). As researchers, we must transgress the rules of academia by showing up to our research fully with our beautiful mess of powerful contradictions, engaging a borderland love ethic that moves us to face our work with nurturing strength, compassion, and renewal.

References

Abrego, L. (2014). *Sacrificing families: Navigating laws, labor and love across borders*. Stanford: Stanford University Press.

Abu-Lughod, J. (1991). Writing against culture. In R. Fox (Ed.), *Recapturing anthropology* (pp. 466–479). Santa Fe: School of American Research Press.

Anzaldúa, G. (1987). *Borderlands: La frontera—the new mestiza*. San Francisco: Aunt Lute Books.

Chang, A. (2011). Undocumented to hyperdocumented: A jornada of protection, papers, and PhD status. *Harvard Educational Review, 81*(3), 508–520.

Chang, A. (2015). Privileged and undocumented: Toward a borderland love ethic. *Association of American Educators, 9*(2), 6–17.

Chavez, K. (2013). *Queer migration politics: Activist rhetoric and coalitional possibilities*. Chicago: University of Illinois Press.

Coll, K. (2004). Necesidades y Problemas: Immigrant Latina vernaculars of belonging, coalition and citizenship in San Francisco, California. *Latino Studies, 2*, 186–209.

Crenshaw, K. W. (1991). Mapping the margins: Intersectionality, identity politics, and violence against women of color. *Stanford Law Review, 43*(6), 1241–1299.

Darder, A. (2003). Teaching as an act of love: Reflections on Paolo Freire and his contributions to our lives and our work. In A. Darder, M. Baltodano, & R. D. Torres (Eds.), *The critical pedagogy reader.* New York: Routledge.

Dowbor, L. (1997). Preface to *pedagogy of the heart* by P. Freire. New York: Continuum.

Freire, P. (1993). *Pedagogy of the city.* New York: Continuum.

Freire, P. (1998). *Pedagogy of freedom: Ethics, democracy, and civic courage.* Lanham: Rowman and Littlefield.

Greenwood, D. J., & Levin, M. (1998). Reform of the social sciences and of universities through action research. In N. Denzin (Ed.), *The handbook of qualitative research* (Vol. 3, pp. 43–64). Thousand Oaks: Sage.

Gutiérrez y Muhs, G., Flores Niemann, Y., González, C. G., & Harris, A. (Eds.). (2012). *Presumed incompetent: The intersections of race and class for women in academia.* Boulder: University Press of Colorado.

Heidbrink, L. (2014). *Migrant Youth, transnational families, and the state: Care and contested interests.* Philadelphia: University of Pennsylvania Press.

hooks, b. (1994). *Teaching to transgress.* New York: Routledge.

hooks, b. (2000). *All about love.* New York: First Perennial.

Jacob, M. (2006). When a native "goes researcher": Notes from the North American indigenous games. *The American Behavioral Scientist, 50*(4), 450–461.

King, Jr., M. L. (1957, November 7). *Loving your enemies.* Delivered at Dexter Avenue Baptist Church Montgomery, Alabama.

Narayan, K. (1993). How native is a "native" anthropologist? *American Anthropological Association, 95*(3), 671–686.

Negrón-Gonzales, G. (2014). Undocumented, unafraid and unapologetic: Re-articulatory practices and migrant youth "illegality". *Latino Studies, 12*(2), 259–278.

Villenas, S. (1996). The colonizer/colonized Chicana ethnographer: Identity, marginalization, and co-optation in the field. *Harvard Educational Review, 66*(4), 711–731.

Zavella, P. (1996). Feminist insider dilemmas: Constructing ethnic identity with Chicana informants. In D. L. Wolf (Ed.), *Feminist dilemmas in fieldwork* (pp. 158–159). Boulder: Westview.

Zinn, M. B. (1979). Field research in minority communities: Ethical, methodological, and political observations by an insider. *Social Problems, 27*(2), 209–219.

CHAPTER 4

Figured Worlds and American Dreams: An Exploration of Agency and Identity Among Undocumented Students

The lives of undocumented Latinx[1] students are at the mercy of the political ups and downs that impact their daily realities. No matter the agentic acts these students take to reach their goals or steps they take to simply survive, there is a limit to what they can achieve in the context of the law. While the unpredictable journey of the DREAM (Development, Relief, and Education for Alien Minors) Act, which sought a conditional pathway to citizenship, raised students' hopes since its inception in 2001, xenophobic messages about undocumented immigrants stealing American jobs, committing crimes, and otherwise abusing the US system of government continue to proliferate. These symbolically violent messages depict undocumented people as uneducated and deficient—as takers of what is not theirs, bringing with them problems rather than contributions.

As a result, undocumented students find themselves on continuously shifting ground, calibrating each decision they make in accordance with or as a strategic reaction to the existing sociopolitical climate. Specifically, some undocumented students find themselves in an ongoing internal battle to fashion an identity that counters the pervasive stereotypes of undocumented people through a process of hyperdocumentation (Chang 2011), while simultaneously bearing the weight of fierce anti-immigrant

---

This article was originally published in 2017 and is reprinted with permission given by the publishers (Chang et al. 2017).

© The Author(s) 2018
A. Chang, *The Struggles of Identity, Education, and Agency in the Lives of Undocumented Students,*
https://doi.org/10.1007/978-3-319-64614-5_4

sentiment. In this chapter, we ask the following questions: How do Latinx undocumented students navigate educational spaces? In what ways do their legal statuses impact the production of their identities? How do they exert agency within the parameters of their undocumented status? In answering these questions, we explore the ways in which some undocumented students *figure*—or take agency in shaping meaning of—their worlds, find identity in their education, and leverage community cultural wealth (Yosso 2005) as a source of critical hope and resilience in their quest to achieve the ever-nebulous American Dream.

LITERATURE REVIEW

Building upon the foundational ideals of the Declaration of Independence, James Truslow Adams (1931) formally introduced and defined the concept of "the American Dream" as "that dream of a land in which life should be better and richer and fuller for everyone, with opportunity for each according to ability or achievement" (pp. 214–215). Nearly a century later, the American Dream is an idea so deeply sewn into the fabric of the United States that its storyline has become internalized as the ethos of the nation. That is, to live in "America" is to belong to a community full of freedom, opportunity, and reward; to be "American" is to honor one's self, family, and country by earning success through individual skill and hard work; and to "live the American Dream" is to enjoy a life of great peace and prosperity as afforded by one's own merits and investments (Hochschild 1995).

This dream—of life in the free and prosperous "America"—has historically influenced immigration trends, luring millions of people in search of a better life to travel to the United States, both legally and illegally. While we acknowledge the racial and cultural diversity that exists among undocumented people in the United States (see Passel and Cohn 2016), this study focuses on Latinx undocumented students. The rationale behind this focus stems, primarily, from the numerical significance of the population. In 2014, approximately 67 percent (7.5 million) of all undocumented persons living in the United States migrated from Mexico and Central America (Passel and Cohn). Furthermore, the geographic proximity of the US/Mexico border (that also extends to Central America) and the United States' contradictory immigration and economic policies with Latin American countries has produced a complex, and often dangerous, social and political climate for Latinx undocumented immigrants both crossing into and living within the United States (Anzaldúa 1987; De Genova 2002; Gonzales 2009; Pérez 2012).

It is at the sociocultural, sociohistorical, and sociopolitical intersection of American Dream ideology and US immigration reality that this study, and the lived experiences of Latinx undocumented students captured herein, must be situated. While certainly not exhaustive, the following review of literature further locates our study within the context of pertinent scholarship on education, identity, and agency. We argue that while most of the existing literature successfully captures the adversity that Latinx students face as undocumented immigrants, our study focuses on the ways in which these students utilize resistance and agency in fostering their identities as undocumented students.

AN OVERVIEW OF UNDOCUMENTED STUDENTS RESEARCH (K-PhD)

Over the past ten years, research around undocumented students, and, more specifically, in research related to the DREAM Act, DREAMers, DACA (Deferred Action for Childhood Arrivals), and "DACAmented" students, has spiked. Accordingly, studies have primarily focused on undergraduate undocumented students and issues within the context of higher education, including in-state tuition policies (Bozick and Miller 2014; Dougherty et al. 2010; Flores 2010; Nguyen and Serna 2014; Vargas 2011) and access to higher education (Diaz-Strong et al. 2011; Huber et al. 2009; Burkhardt et al. 2012; Chávez et al. 2007; Gonzales 2009; Garcia and Tierney 2011; Pérez and Rodriguez 2011; Pérez 2010a, b). Studies have also examined academic performance and issues of recruiting, admitting, and retaining undocumented students (Abrego 2006; Enriquez 2011; Gonzales 2010; Pérez 2010a, b; Pérez and Rodriguez 2011; Rincon 2010; Ryscavage and Canaris 2013), with a particular interest in these students' successful navigation of academia (Contreras 2009; Dozier 2001; Flores and Horn 2009; Garcias and Tierney 2011; Pérez et al. 2009). Studies within the field of higher education have also looked beyond the horizon of college graduation to better understand the poignant issue of undocumented students' options for post-secondary paths (e.g., graduate school, employment, careers)—or lack thereof (Abrego and Gonzales 2010; Jacobs and Ochoa 2011; Abrego and Gonzales 2010; López 2010; Ortiz and Hinojosa 2010; Rodriguez and Cruz 2009).

Research has also emerged about the academic experiences of undocumented students, particularly focusing on those who are academically successful (Covarrubias and Lara 2014; Enriquez 2011; Gonzales 2010; Pérez et al. 2009; Lopez 2010; Viramontez Anguiano and Lopez 2012). Meanwhile, other provocative pieces of research have honed in on the legal impacts, challenges, and implications of undocumented status (Abrego 2006, 2008, 2011; Menjívar and Abrego 2009; Coutin 2010, 2011a, b; Olivas 2012; Román 2013). In their comprehensive overview of the possibilities and challenges that immigrant children face in US K-12 public schools, Suárez-Orozco et al. (2010) laid a foundation for the imminent work awaiting scholars of immigrant students: drawing attention to the "less than optimal" (p. 88) conditions that immigrant students face and advocating policies necessary for them to become successful students and flourishing people. These conditions include the lack of emotional and academic support from schools and the violent and sometimes toxic nature of school environments. Pérez' (2009, 2012) and Gonzales' (2009) work on undocumented Latinx students has been groundbreaking in capturing the "legal paradox" (Gonzales 2009, p. 25) and educational obstacles students must navigate to pursue higher education because of their undocumented status. Additionally, some scholars have theorized around undocumented experiences as it relates to hyperdocumentation (Chang 2011), deportability in everyday life (De Genova 2002), identity development (Ellis and Chen 2013), constructing citizenship (Coutin 2010, 2013; Glenn 2011), race, spatialization, borderlands, and "illegality" (Coutin 2003, 2005; De Genova 2005, 2006; De Genova and Ramos-Zayas 2003; De Genova and Peutz 2010).

IDENTITY, EDUCATION, AND AGENCY IN UNDOCUMENTED STUDENTS' LIVES

The exploration of identity, education, and agency within the lives of undocumented students has been spearheaded by various scholars. Muñoz (2015) documented the journey stories of undocumented and unafraid community activists in her groundbreaking book on identity and social activism, exploring how undocumented students make meaning of their legal status within the contexts of higher education and social activism. Drawing from the foundational work of scholars such as Abrego (2011), De Genova (2002, 2005), Galindo (2012), Gonzales (2008, 2011), Muñoz and Maldonado (2012), Negrón-Gonzales (2014), Nicholls (2013), Pérez and Cortés (2011), and Huber (2010), Muñoz introduced the concept of *critical legal consciousness*, an awareness that undocumented social activists use to gain new knowledge about their legality as well as a tool to critique policies that directly affect undocumented students. As Muñoz (2015) noted, the counternarratives presented by these scholars illustrate how "youth have strategically constructed their own compelling messages, highlighting not only their pride in being undocumented, unafraid and unapologetic, but also how this adopted identity informs and shapes their other social identities" (p. 7). Indeed, undocumented students' identities sit at the crux of intersectionality (Crenshaw 1989, 1991) incorporating identities such as sexuality, race, culture, socioeconomic status, religion, national origin, language, and immigration status.

The aforementioned literature appropriately demonstrated that at every fork in their lives' roads, there were painful limits to the extent to which they could advocate for their own futures. It also bore witness to the fact that many students became politically active in local, state, and national efforts as "DREAMers"; many shed their cloaks of invisibility and silence to proclaim themselves "undocumented and unafraid"; and many maintained critical hope and otherwise behaved in ways that affirmed their success as cultural citizens even in the face of seemingly impossible odds. What we do not know is how these students—on a daily, hourly, and even moment-to-moment basis—managed to cultivate and enact such agency while entrenched in a process of interpreting, integrating, internalizing, and interjecting themselves as worthy objects within competing worlds of hope and despair. Thus, we are left to question how undocumented students are able to actively participate in such different cultural worlds from within their socially constructed and scripted social positions. So while substantive research, as evidenced in this review, has explored the everyday barriers to and complexities of undocumented students' educational paths "with the law or against the law" (Abrego 2011, p. 360) as well as their identity development within this context, this study primarily focused on the ways in which some undocumented students *figure*—or take agency in shaping meaning of—their worlds, find identity in their education, and leverage community cultural wealth (Yosso 2005) as a source of critical hope and resilience in their quest to achieve the mythological American Dream.

METHODOLOGY

This chapter draws from a qualitative study of 18 diverse students, ages 18 and above, who identified as undocumented or once undocumented to address the following research questions: How do Latinx undocumented students navigate educational spaces? In what ways do their legal statuses impact the production of their identities? How do they exert agency within the parameters of their undocumented status? Participants were recruited via e-mail invitation and through the snowball sampling method (Patton 1990), and data were collected through semi-structured interviews (Fontana and Frey 2000). Because of the vulnerable legal status of this population, we paid particular attention to confidentiality, paying special care to the importance of rapport, a component that is "essential in helping to create for the participant the feeling of being respected and of being genuinely heard" (Madison 2005, p. 31). While we were interested in the findings of this research, we understood that our primary responsibility was to those studied. As Madison (2005) noted: "This responsibility supersedes the goal of knowledge, completion of project, and obligation to funders and sponsors" (p. 111).

We conducted open-ended interviews Madison (2005), each lasting between 45 and 90 minutes. All interviews were digitally audio-recorded with participant permission, and pseudonyms were used in documenting the data.

Data Analysis

After data were collected, the interviews were transcribed and uploaded to Crocodoc, an embedded HTML5 document viewer that allows multiple users to annotate a single document. Each interview transcript was coded by each of us using an open coding method, tracking our coding through the insertion of comments (explaining the code) directly linked to specific quotations within the transcripts. We followed inductive data analysis throughout the data-collection process (Lincoln and Guba 1985). We created codes to characterize participants' comments, reviewed each code, and compared them to make sure each was relatively unique and that they encompassed fairly heterogeneous codes. We produced a list of 88 supercodes with an average of three subcodes per supercode. Following this process, we reviewed the codes. We analyzed both commonalities and variations among the codes. Codes that related to the same content were grouped together in "provisional categories" (Lincoln and Guba 1985, p. 347) by collaboratively identifying emerging code patterns or dominant themes. The identification of emerging code patterns or dominant themes allowed us to capture central key narratives that rose to the surface. From these coding patterns, we identified identity, education, and agency as major themes. We identified specific participant quotes that illustrated these themes and, from there, discussed the meaning and implications of these quotes. After discussing the quotes with one another through the course of five one-hour meetings, we revisited the quotations to ensure that we didn't overlook any significant ones. Finally, we developed subthemes that eventually served as our findings.

Several studies have utilized undocumented students' narratives of various ages including children and adolescents (King and Punti 2012; Patel 2013), young adults (Arriaga 2012; Castro-Salazar and Bagley 2010; Galindo 2011, 2012; Hernandez et al. 2011; Huber and Malagon 2007; Huber 2010; Torres and Wicks-Asbun 2014), and college students/adults (Bagley and Castro-Salazar 2012; Chang 2011; Jacobo and Ochoa 2011; Orner 2008; Pérez 2009). Program case studies both in K-12 (Chen et al. 2010; Rodriquez and Cruz 2009; Storlie and Jach 2012) and higher education (Bagley and Castro-Salazar 2012; Enriquez 2014; Nienhusser 2014) have also served as methodological tools to understand the educational experiences of undocumented students. This study follows the methodological lead of such studies and at the same time uses an original theoretical framework for the first time, as a lens to approaching these experiences.

THEORETICAL FRAMEWORK

Abes (2009) boldly demonstrated that "All theoretical perspectives that guide research are incomplete" (p. 141), providing evidence that more nuanced examinations are particularly essential to unveiling hidden power structures in research on student learning and development. Abes' discussion of "theoretical borderlands" specifically calls attention to the ways theory, when void of critical perspectives, often neglects the reality and influence of systematic oppression on human development—an oversight that can inappropriately frame already marginalized populations as developmentally stunted or otherwise deficient. This work adds to a growing movement toward research that employs what Kincheloe and McLaren (2005) termed theoretical "bricolage"—or the layering of multiple perspectives—to surface inherent complexities in the creation of knowledge and its translation to practice.

Holland et al.'s (1998) social practice theory of self and identity resists a history of paradigmatic isolation and instead positions the development of personhood, or identity, as an essential and continuous human experience that is most visible through both anthropological and social constructivist lenses. Building upon the work of foundational social psychologist G.H. Mead, the theory constructs a supplementary relationship between critical, cultural, and social constructivist perspectives for a critical, social-psychological examination of identity that more accurately captures lived experience. Therefore, we draw on Holland et al.'s (1998) social practice theory of self and identity as a framework to make meaning of student narratives, specifically employing the concepts of *figured worlds, positional/ relational identities, space of authoring and play, improvisational activity.* The following sections provide an overview of the theory's critical utility in unveiling the dynamic and continuous process of social-psychological exchanges between individuals and their environments that is inherent to human social interaction.

Positional/Relational Identity

The social practice theory of self and identity centers the role of self-objectification: how an individual interprets and *figures* herself or himself as an object in a social world (Holland et al. 1998). The authors explained, "People tell others who they are, but even more important, they tell themselves and then try to act as though they are who they say they are" (Holland et al., p. 3). It is through this process of "self-fashioning" that an individual forms, performs, and evolves *positional/relational identity.* Relational identities "...have to do with behavior as indexical of claims to social relationships with others. They have to do with how one identifies one's position relative to others, mediated through the ways one feels comfortable or constrained" (Holland et al., p. 127). Positional identities "have to do with the day-to-day and on-the-ground relations of power, deference and entitlement, social affiliation and distance—with the social-interactional, social-relational structures of the lived world" (Holland et al., p. 127). The interactive figuring of a positional/relational identity embeds the self in continuous social practice, and serves as a primary mediator of human social behavior.

Space of Authoring and Play

Holland et al. (1998) further theorized that "no human action is singularly expressive" (p. 169); rather, it is always a product of ongoing inner dialogue where identities are never static and ever forming. There is a *space of authoring* that is therefore "invisible to itself" (p. 173) because the self is a continuous activity and cannot be finalized or captured. Additionally, this space of authoring is not immune from hegemonic norms and structures, which insidiously permeate both our cognitive processes and actions. It is a space where, in any precise moment, an identity is asserted—partially self-orchestrated, but also bound by social parameters and sites that simultaneously constrain language and expression: the very resources utilized to devise such an identity. *Play* is "the medium of mastery, indeed of creation of ourselves as human actors. Without the capacity to formulate other social scenes in imagination, there can be little force to a sense of self, little agency" (p. 236). It is precisely within the dialectical processes of authoring and play that this study locates the site of Latinx student identity production.

Improvisational Activity

The social practice theory of self and identity (Holland et al. 1998) is founded on the notion that one has the capability to actively participate in different cultural worlds within one's socially constructed and scripted social position. Furthermore, the theory describes a dialectical relationship between social history and identity formation and centers engagement in such relationship as the primary mechanism for human agency:

> Thus persons and, to a lesser extent, groups are caught in the tensions between past histories that have settled in them and the present discourses and images that attract them and somehow impinge upon them. In this continuous self-fashioning, identities are hard-won standpoints that, however dependent on social support and however vulnerable to change, make at least a modicum of self-direction possible. They are possibilities for mediating agency. (p. 4)

That is, there are spaces that remain somewhat maneuverable "even as these identities are worked and reworked on the social landscape" (Holland et al., p. 270). This maneuvering, or the ways in which people actively participate in social worlds, is referred to as *improvisational activity* and describes one's "responses to social and cultural openings and impositions" (Holland et al., p. 270). Improvisation, then, is the central mechanism connecting identity production and behavior, allowing for the elaboration of identities despite socially imposed constraints; it is the predominant form of social agency within one's life context and position.

Figured Worlds

It is from positional/relational identities, within spaces of authoring and play, and through improvisational activity that figured worlds are continuously imagined, enacted, and evolved. Figured worlds are simultaneously the meta-process and product of the social practice theory of self and identity (Holland et al. 1998), described as:

> historical phenomena, to which we are recruited or into which we enter, which themselves develop through the works of their participants. Figured worlds, like activities, are not so much things or objects to be apprehended, as processes or traditions of apprehension which gather us up and give us form as our lives intersect them. (p. 41)

Moreover, they are metanarratives that develop over time and history—continually forming—and born from social locations, subjectivities, and interactions. These narratives "rest upon people's abilities to form and be formed in collectively realized 'as if' realms" (Holland et al., p. 49): the dynamic, interwoven fabric between actors and plot, history and presence, social construction and individual agency. Figured worlds supply "the contexts of meaning for actions, cultural productions, performances, disputes, for the understandings that people develop to direct their own behavior in these worlds" (Holland et al., p. 60).

Therefore, figured worlds are both imagined communities and lived realities that operate dialectically and dialogically. They are spaces simultaneously confined by hidden power structures and malleable through authoring, play, and improvisation. They are defined by the ways individuals participate in relation to and with these worlds on a daily basis. Most importantly, they are "historically contingent, socially enacted, culturally constructed worlds" (Holland et al. 1998, p. 7) rooted in the essential and continuous human experience: the development of identity, or personhood. The social practice theory of self and identity (Holland et al.) maintains that there is always space for agency within one's life context and position. Thus, the continuous process of figuring worlds serves as the primary mechanism of agency in and liberation from reproduced and imposed social landscapes.

In this chapter, we leverage the power of human voice and storytelling to examine the ways in which undocumented Latinx students cultivate and leverage positional/relational identities, find meaning and solace in spaces of authoring and play, and engage in improvisational activity to confront, construct, and ultimately refigure their everyday experiences within "American worlds." We invoke the Latin American tradition of *testimonios*, as both a guiding theory and method, that empowers participants "to put the scattered pieces together of a painful experience in a new way that generates wisdom and consciousness" (Cervantes-Soon 2012, p. 374). Through these critical narratives, we are invited by participants to explore the figured spaces of self and identity that undocumented Latinx students iteratively fashion and navigate within their everyday lives, while in the pursuit of the American Dream.

FINDINGS

Across the interviews, participant *testimonios* supported extant scholarship identifying barriers to the academic and personal success of undocumented Latinx students. However, what also surfaced were dynamic and nuanced narratives of battles waged—both internally and externally—to navigate and resist the monolithic identity and misconceptions projected onto undocumented people. At times, students were immobilized by fear, risk, challenge, silence, and defeat; and at other times, they were propelled by courage, responsibility, community, choice, and hope. The following sections introduce two primary themes, and their interrelationship, emergent from the data: (1) Adversity as an Undocumented American and (2) Community Cultural Wealth and Collective Resistance.

Adversity as an Undocumented American

Participants' reflections on their experiences with adversity were either associated with an external challenge (i.e., connected to living and interacting socially) or an internal challenge (i.e., connected to making meaning of themselves and their social realities). Externally, participants described the restrictions and complexity associated with "illegality" (Abrego 2014), and the difficulty inherent to navigating socially hostile environments rooted in widespread ignorance and misconceptions. Relatedly, participants also shared their internal struggles to reject the monolithic identity projected onto them (i.e., "illegal," "undocumented") and their attempts to find and/or fashion unique identities of their own.

Illegality Abrego (2014) defined the concept of illegality as "the condition of immigrants' legal status and deportability" (p. 7), specifically tracing US illegality back to restrictive legislation enacted in the early 1980s to enforce borders and criminalize undocumented immigrants in the workforce. All participants detailed several ways illegality, or being undocumented, manifested in their daily social lives; many times stifling, stunting, or altogether stopping their engagement in Western-normative "coming of age" rituals, such as obtaining a driver's license, finding a job, and applying for college or financial aid. In particular, the intersection of social class and illegality emerged in many interviews, highlighting a common experience of compounded stressors and marginalization among undocumented students.

Katerina's transcripts capture the essence of the tremendous complexity and tangled hardships of illegality as experienced by multiple participants in this study. In sharing the story of her family's immigration and subsequent deportation, Katerina's narrative calls attention to the powerful ways undocumented status can impact a single family:

INTERVIEWER:	Did you have any idea why your family decided to immigrate here?
KATERINA:	Yeah. My parents, both my mom and dad, came without me first. They went to Miami. They worked there for a while and then my mom went back to get me. It was because she's a doctor in Nicaragua. It still wasn't very good pay. My dad; he was a civil engineer, but he wasn't really working in that field. They both decided to maybe come here and make money, but it ended becoming more permanent.
INTERVIEWER:	Were your parents able to still practice their careers here?
KATERINA:	No. My mom; she was a janitor at a school, and my dad just worked in construction...Well, in 2009 my dad was actually deported back to Nicaragua. My mom continued working at the school until I graduated high school. I was a sophomore in high school when he was deported. When I graduated high school, my mom and my little sister both went back to Nicaragua.
INTERVIEWER:	Tell me about what it was like to have your dad deported and then your mom and sister move back.
KATERINA:	It was really hard. The hardest part, I think was when my dad left because he was the main...income... Financially, everything changed. I had to work. I had

to start to pick a part-time job in high school, just to help out. Like pay for my own stuff, I guess. Then when my mom left, I just had to become an adult really quickly. She decided to leave because I was accepted to [large public university], and I won a four-year scholarship. She just thought it would be better if I stayed instead of going to school over there... I've had to become independent really quickly. Like, the scholarship I got was is only for tuition. So, I have to pay rent, books, and everything else out of my pocket. So, I've been working like 30 hours a week since my freshman year.

For most participants, hyperdocumentation (Chang 2011)—the inordinate acquisition of *papeles*, or documentation "papers"—was viewed as a penultimate need to reposition them with greater legal rights and protection. However, one participant's reflection evidences how illegality can remain symbolically powerful in the lives of immigrant students even upon a change of status:

It's just really weird because I have this piece of paper and this nine-digit number that I have been waiting for my whole life. It was really weird. The whole process itself was really kind of—the word that comes to mind when I think about the immigration process was just...cold. (DOLORES)

Interview data provide strong evidence that illegality surfaced as the primary factor mediating participant experiences. However, beyond a direct confrontation of structural and legal limitations, illegality also seemed to permeate cultural domains and emerged as a stealth instigator of hostility and social stigma toward undocumented immigrants.

Hostility Supporting extant scholarship on the experiences of undocumented, participant *testimonios* were situated within complex and, at times, hostile social climates founded upon culturally produced notions of illegality. One participant vividly recounted being confronted by peer hostility in the public setting of a college classroom:

I remember this one experience in a class. It might not have been the scariest experience but it made me feel like I could not come out. I sat in the middle of the classroom, and we would write notes about the videos we watched.

No one put their names on them, but because I was in the middle, all of them collected on my desk. So, I was able to read what people were writing. There was one note that was written in blue cursive; it came from the side of the room where this one white man sat. It said, we were talking about the economy, and it was like "It's all of the illegals. It's their fault and we're doomed and, you know, we should just kick them out." Those are the little reminders that made me realize, "This is not a safe place."' (GRACE)

Despite feeling hurt and emotionally triggered, Grace coached herself to remain silent out of her fear of being exposed and shamed: "Okay. Calm down because they're gonna figure out that you're undocumented, and then you're gonna get accused."

The option to be silent in the presence of risk and fear surfaced across participant interviews as a situationally contingent choice of action motivated by survival instinct. As Enrique explained, "A lot of students—a lot of undocumented students don't ask for help because they are afraid or they don't feel comfortable." Dolores also recalled a hostile experience with a tenured faculty member in her academic department. When Dolores expressed that she was struggling with a class paper, the faculty member simply told her to drop the class, and then systematically removed Dolores from the course without her consent. Despite her outrage at the inappropriate behavior of the professor, Dolores recognized that an escalation of the situation could potentially result in greater complications, or an altogether detriment, to her ultimate aim of college completion: "She was like the tenured professor and the chair in the department! I don't want to get on her bad side. I'll just take the hit and take the class again—and that will be that."

Misconceptions of Identity As participants reflected on their experiences with illegality and social hostility, they described an underlying dominant culture of ignorance, or lack of awareness, regarding the realities of being undocumented in America. Enrique, a light-skinned, green-eyed participant, disclosed one experience in which a peer explicitly asked him "Oh, how come you don't look like other Mexicans?" While not all misconceptions surfaced as overtly as in the situation with Enrique, participants identified ways in which they felt misunderstood and/or stereotyped. For example, Daniela perceived her peers to make false assumptions regarding undocumented student receipt of government support:

[People believe undocumented immigrants are]...leeching off the government, that you get free everything—which isn't true at all. They don't even know that you can't apply for financial aid; you can't apply for things like insurance. They think that you get welfare money and just, money-wise, that the government supports you—but that's not true, not at all. (DANIELA)

Enrique revisited his experiences with peer misconceptions and expressed frustration with their ignorance, or lack of awareness, of his lived experience as an undocumented student:

> You know for example, a lot of undocumented students that I know can't afford to live on campus or have to work on top of going to school in order to help their families or even themselves because we can't get financial aid. It's definitely one of the challenges people don't realize or even imagine. (ENRIQUE)

Moreover, Enrique's reactions to peer privileges and misconceptions embody both the offensive (anger, frustration) and defensive mechanisms triggered in participants during such encounters:

> For example for me, I have never had the luxury, I guess, of failing any of my classes. I have had friends that, in college, it's easy for them to say that they are not going to go to class or that they failed a class and can take it again. But for me it's definitely not an option because, for one, I feel like there's a little bit more of a need to prove myself because of my undocumented status. So later when applying for a job and also money-wise I don't have the money to sort of like retake classes over and over again. (ENRIQUE)

As captured in Daniela's and Enrique's interviews, participants experienced frequent assaults on their identity. More specifically, they discussed the significant challenge of feeling continuously essentialized by unfounded stereotypes. They experienced being pegged with a monolithic identity of "undocumented."

COMMUNITY CULTURAL WEALTH AND COLLECTIVE RESISTANCE

As evidenced within the previous sections, data from this study validate literature that positions undocumented Latinx students in complex socio-cultural contexts of adversity. Participant *testimonios* commonly centered on the interplay of identity and agency, and specifically the opportunity and responsibility to debunk the myth of the undocumented as a monolith (i.e., the deviant, uneducated, incompetent, and unwelcome immigrant). These students also acknowledged that maintaining hope and motivation in the face of adversity is exhausting and defeating at times given the tremendous hardships and sacrifices. Yet even when faced with extraordinary barriers to academic, personal, and professional success, participants exhibited resilience, engaged in active forms of individual and collective resistance, and—most remarkably—maintained critical hope for and investment in their own chance at achieving the American Dream. They hurdled barriers and transcended the confines placed upon them by xenophobia and illegality; and they did not succumb to the stress.

We were compelled to explore how these students were able to demonstrate such resilience and sustained resistance and found that community, or collectivism, emerged as an essential asset and source of support in participants' short- and long-term success and well-being. This finding is supported by Tara Yosso's (2005) framework of community cultural wealth. Grounded in critical race theory, the concept of community cultural wealth (Yosso 2005) challenges traditional (i.e., white) interpretations of power and capital (Bourdieu 1986), which often position People of Color as "deficient," to instead acknowledge the collective "wealth" contained within Communities of Color. Moreover, through her pivotal work, Yosso rejects dominant, hyperindividualistic examinations of power and highlighted the unique resources, skills, strengths, and ways of knowing People of Color both bring from and nurture within their communities:

1. **Aspirational capital:** the ability to maintain hopes and dreams for the future, even in the face of real and perceived barriers.
2. **Linguistic capital:** includes the intellectual and social skills attained through communication experiences in more than one language and/or style.
3. **Familial capital:** those cultural knowledges nurtured among *familia* (kin) that carry a sense of community history, memory, and cultural intuition (Bernal 1998, 2002).
4. **Social capital:** networks of people and community resources. These peer and other social contacts can provide both instrumental and emotional support to navigate through society's institutions (Gilbert 1982; Stanton-Salazar 2001).
5. **Navigational capital:** skills of maneuvering through social institutions.
6. **Resistant capital:** those knowledges and skills fostered through oppositional behavior that challenges inequality (Bernal 1997; Freire 1970, 1973; Giroux 1983; McLaren 1993; Solórzano and Delgado Bernal 2001).

In analyzing participant interview transcripts, we found evidence of all six forms of cultural wealth, which manifested in three strategies: (1) defiance, (2) collective reciprocity, and (3) critical hope.

Defiance As captured within the subtheme *misconceptions of identity,* participants voiced sincere frustration, if not anger, toward being essentialized. Although the subtheme of *defiance* is presented here as separate from the aforementioned themes capturing adversity (i.e., *illegality, hostility, misconceptions of identity*), they were inseparable for participants. It was immediately apparent that these students experienced pain, shame, and anger when they perceived themselves or their community to be misunderstood and/or inappropriately defined by stereotypes, and their feelings were channeled into acts of resistance, or defiance: intentional behaviors and courses of action to defy false assumptions and unfair expectations of undocumented people. Even in revisiting previously shared excerpts of participant interviews, it is evident that individuals simultaneously named the individual stress experienced as a result of hostile interactions or misconceptions of identity and illustrated a strong, collective commitment to dispelling stereotypes and resisting defeat. Moreover, in considering Yosso's (2005) framework of community cultural wealth, students articulated unique and intricate weavings of navigational, linguistic, and resistant capitals to engage in defiance.

For example, within the context of sharing his frustration with the privileged behaviors of documented Americans, Enrique also acknowledged his community responsibility to defy assumptions: "...I feel like there's a little more proving myself because of my undocumented status." When Grace felt slandered and scapegoated in class as a "problematic illegal," she coached herself to manage the emotions she experienced so that she could present herself in a manner that would maintain her power and safety, while also preventing her from becoming vulnerable to further attacks:

> I knew the professor might be safe, but the classroom, the students that I'm with in the classroom were not. I remember like...feeling hot. Then thinking, like, "Okay. Calm down because they're gonna figure out that you're undocumented and then you're gonna get accused." (GRACE)

And, despite being separated from her family and experiencing tremendous financial hardship, Katerina opted to work and continue with her education, alone, in the United States. During her interview, she focused on the positive outcome of her hard work and resilience: "So, I've been working like 30 hours a week since my freshman year. But, I don't have any student loans, so I guess that's the good part of it—I'll graduate on time without any debt."

Although participants described feeling stigmatized by unfounded stereotypes projected onto undocumented people, participants also described rejecting such projections of a socially scripted, monolithic identity. Most notably, when asked to discuss how being undocumented shaped their day-to-day experiences, many participants were quick to intentionally differentiate their lack of US citizenship as a *status*, not a form of identity, and placed as minimal focus as possible on their status:

> So as far I mean, identifying with it, I mean I don't really. Like, I mean I am undocumented. I don't think that's an identity feature of someone. It's just like a lack of a piece of paper. So it's more of a burden than a piece of who I am really. (ALEJANDRO).
>
> How do I define myself? As an intellectual. I love learning, and I love school. (GRACE)
>
> My daily life? I don't really think about it because this is my life. I've basically lived this way my entire life and, because, in a way I feel like I belong here because I've been here so long. (DANIELA)

However, participants did acknowledge identifying with undocumented people as a collective and social movement and specifically discussed how being undocumented shaped their values, passions, and actions. Chavo described this affiliation as initially, and commonly, unstated: "There were just five of us. We were basically a cohort of our own because we knew we weren't like the rest of the students."

Despite rejecting "undocumented" as an individual feature of their identity, participants felt interconnected with other undocumented students through their common battles with illegality and, as a result, described a shared responsibility and commitment to engage in defiance. Pepe specifically commented on the perception that undocumented people, as a group, are often associated with having lesser intellectual ability than those who are documented: "There are a lot of bright people out there, especially undocumented people." He extended this defense by adding:

> I mean, there are a lot of engineers that have graduated and can't do engineering in their field because they don't have papers. There are undocumented students that could be doctors right now if they had papers. There are people that want to work for the FBI. There are people who want to

work for the White House. There are people that wanna be senators, that wanna be legislator—but they can't because they don't have papers. (PEPE)

Pepe's statement exemplifies the tension undocumented students must navigate on a daily basis—that between socially imposed illegality and individual and collective motivation and aspiration. During his interview, Pepe named several highly respected professions with skill sets and competencies that require post-secondary and advanced degrees. He also indicated a sincere familiarity with undocumented individuals who have traversed the educational terrain to successfully complete the credentialing necessary to serve in these respected positions and professions, each of which stands in stark contrast to those stereotyped to Latinx people (i.e., menial jobs such as hospitality workers, gardeners, construction workers). Finally, he called attention to the ways illegality systematically impedes undocumented persons, individually, and undocumented people, collectively, from pursuing their true aspirations—situations incorrectly perceived by dominant society as "failures" that only deepen stereotypes. Like Pepe, many participants weaved together linguistic and resistant forms of capital to chip away at the false images plastered onto undocumented people and construct a more accurate counternarrative—one that depicts undocumented people as resilient fighters for their individual dreams and their collective community's well-being. Linguistic capital manifested itself through the participants' careful social performances; the intentional selection of their word choice and communication styles and expressions, adoption and ownership of an academic/intellectual identity, cautious decision-making around self-disclosure of legal status, and recognition of the power and legitimacy achieved through the mastery of the English language. Thus, undocumented students used defiance as a strategy to defy misconceptions and as a vehicle to honor individual aspirations, community responsibility, and collective reciprocity.

Collective Reciprocity Participants commonly framed their acts of defiance as both individually and collectively beneficial, with specific emphasis placed on the idea of community responsibility: feeling compelled to transform the image of undocumented people. In this sense, students perceived their individual success, or defiance, as a strategy to contribute to and pave new paths for their community—nurturing and advancing the motivations, aspirations, and hopes of the collective. As Pepe shared, "...they see that motivation in us: even though we hit walls, they see us get up from them." Moreover, data also exhibited how participants simultaneously relied upon community support to engage in these same acts of defiance, which were in return aimed at supporting the community. Collective reciprocity defines this interrelationship in which individuals pull from familial and social capitals, both present and historical, to summon internal motivation, resilience, and wisdom in their journeys to navigate and resist cultural and systematic illegality—with each success immediately reinvested back into the community's collective power.

Most tangibly, participants centered the role of relationships (e.g., familial, social) in their individual processes of resilience and resistance. Across the interviews, students consistently discussed the presence and support of their families, or lack thereof, as inextricably linked to their other forms of capital, such as aspirational, navigational, and resistant. For example, both Grace and Katerina attributed their educational drive and persistence to the experiences of their parents:

> My mother, well, both of my parents, actually, have been very insistent on me going to college. That [not going] was never gonna be an option. They both wanted to be teachers at one point. So, education has always been part of growing up, part of who I am. (GRACE)
>
> I think a lot of has been like the fact that I'm by myself and I don't have my family with me. That's always been my constant motivator; that since my family sacrificed a lot for me when they left, I kind of have to prove to them that I can do it. (KATERINA)

While disclosing how their families contributed to their individual success, many participants also connected, or projected, their aspirations to future generations of immediate and culturally extended circles of family:

> I saw that there was a lot of responsibility for me to continue my Master's program; it's more or less that I want to pave a path for my younger cousins and nieces. Like, I want him to know it's not impossible to keep on going, especially when you find something that you're passionate about. (CHAVO)
>
> That's been my new motivation to finish school, is to help others, especially the Latino community. Especially here in Wyoming, which I mean is growing. Immigration in Wyoming is growing. (PEPE)

Both Chavo and Pepe posited that their struggles to overcome obstacles led them to use their experiences to help others in similar positions. That is, they transformed their experiences of indignation into sources of motivation and strength to help others, thus shifting the discourse of undocumented students from rejection and restriction to growth and progress. Furthermore, the juxtaposition of Grace, Katerina, Chavo, and Pepe's narratives highlights an intergenerational elasticity to community wealth in which cultural knowledges, values, and motivations are connected through history and carried forward from past to present to future generations through relationship (i.e., familial networks).

Socially, participants also cited peer and educational relationships (e.g., teacher/professor, counselor) as important sources of support and guidance, whether through acts of empathy and emotional support, advice on navigating legal and logistical complexities as a student, or simple gestures of human solidarity. For example, a defining moment for Chavo came unexpectedly from his sixth-grade teacher: "He [said to us], 'I don't care where you're from, who you are—you're all equal in this class, and I will teach you as such.'" Chavo further reflected on his educational journey, poignantly recalling his struggle to cope with the death of his mother and regain the motivation to learn:

> I think a lot of what helped me with learning wasn't the instructional part; it was more of the emotional support from teachers. When teachers cared about me, I felt a lot more responsibility to try to do well in my classes. (CHAVO)

Social and familial forms of capital were similarly described by a few other participants from a point of tension between losing and gaining support. When asked what supported her journey, Katerina shared:

> I think psychology, for one. My dad was deported. So, in high school I became really close with my high school counselor. She kind of helped me get through a lot of things. Then, I just kind of wanted to be here. I wanted to be a counselor. (KATERINA)

Finally, Dolores captured the mediating and dynamic effects these forms of connection to community had on participants' success as students, and called attention to the potential consequence of a shift, or transition, in academic support:

> I think [I was successful in high school] because I had a lot of support from my teachers in high school. You know, once I actually got to college, I think that was a little different for me. I kind of noticed that my academic performance started to drop. So I guess I think it's about like support—whether that comes from educators, family, or friends. But, I definitely think that educators and the school part of it play a large role. (DOLORES)

Critical Hope It is evident that, despite unique circumstances and contexts, each participant established a significant, if not definitive, relationship to community characterized by a reciprocal flow of strength and support. As displayed by the previously presented excerpts, the kinds of support participants received from community ranged from instructional to emotional. However, one universal, reciprocally exchanged form of community support emerged in the data: hope. More specifically, interview transcripts documented a presence of *critical* hope, which West (2008) defined as rejecting both the despair of hopelessness and the false hopes of "cheap American optimism" (p. 41). Instead, critical hope demands a committed and active struggle "against the evidence in order to change the deadly tides of wealth inequality, group xenophobia, and personal despair" (West 2004, pp. 296–297).

Critical hope surfaced as both a means to transgress the futility of reality and the essential structure of support undergirding these students' sustained resilience and resistance, both individually and as a collective. That is, critical hope served participants as both a coping mechanism and an act of defiance in and of itself. Most visibly, critical hope manifested in participants' sustained commitment to pursuing their dreams, or what Yosso (2005) might consider aspirational capital: "My dreams? I just started this year in my Master's program at Higher Education Leadership. I hope to also pursue a doctorate in the higher education field" (CHAVO).

Similar to Chavo's declaration, participants imagined bold dreams for their futures within the United States, despite the complexity and adversity characterizing their daily experiences as undocumented persons. While the act of dreaming alone could be a form of "false hope" (Duncan-Andrade 2009), participants also articulated the personal strategies they were enacting to remain in active pursuit of such aspirations. Most commonly, participants cited education as their primary vehicle for and symbol of critical hope, and believed their path to citizenship was directly connected to academic success: "If you have the best grades, if you are the best of the best, maybe then you'll get papers" (FLOR). In this sense, formal education served to cultivate a material form of hope in which participants were given the resources to "deal with the forces that affect their lives" (Syme 2004, p. 3).

According to participants, trying one's best and being a top student leads to greater scholarship eligibility and access to higher education, which in turn increases the possibility of gaining "papers," or becoming a legal citizen. Participants exhibited significant investment in their "American Dreams" and channeled that conviction into their educational drive. During Yaelisa's interview, she narrated her journey to higher education and attributed her resilience and success in navigating the barriers of illegality to critical hope. Yaelisa described her first confrontation with her legal status during high school; after a visit from college counselors, she realized she could not apply for financial aid or certain scholarships and colleges without a Social Security number.

INTERVIEWER: How did you feel when you found out that you couldn't apply?

YAELISA: I felt that I couldn't fulfill my dreams anymore. I felt sad. I kind of felt disappointed. I don't know with whom or with what but I was disappointed... I still had hope though. I always had hope and faith. Even though I knew that I needed the loan or financial aid from the government, I still researched for scholarships that didn't require the social security number.

Despite initial feelings of doubt, Yaelisa drew upon, and demonstrated, critical hope to fuel her fight for access to higher education—further validating the symbiotic relationship between aspirational, navigational, and resistant forms of capital (Yosso 2005). Yaelisa also shared how hope enabled her to take important risks and keep searching for possibilities despite great odds:

> I applied for a scholarship in my freshman year that required a social [security number]. I don't know why, but I applied for it and I passed the interview and they somehow gave me the scholarship! My parents and I decided it was a miracle—that they are helping us and they are making an exception. (YAELISA)

Maintaining critical hope pushed Yaelisa to challenge the system of illegality and, in return, her success re-inspired her sense of hope:

> I used to think that maybe I can't [go to college], but I'm still going to do my best to be a top student—because that would help later on. Because, like I said, there are scholarships that don't require a social security number and most of them do require that you have a good academic standing. (YAELISA)

Yaelisa shared that it was only because she continued taking risks that she ultimately was able to obtain multiple scholarships and successfully enroll in college. While concluding her story, Yaelisa also demonstrated a responsibility to other undocumented students by "paying forward" the navigational capital she gained through her own journey:

> So, when I was in college already, I knew this other student that also applied for the same scholarship [that I had received]. She asked me, "how did you do it with the [name of foundation] scholarship?" She told me that they [undocumented peers] said I was the first one that knew how to navigate the system. (YAELISA)

Yaelisa's story is only one of many similar stories shared across participant interviews. However, it is a powerful exemplar of the cyclical pattern universally described by the students in this study: undocumented communities cultivate and nurture a foundation of critical hope within their youth, who are then empowered to be resilient, resistant, and defiant as successful students, which ultimately reinvests in their *collective* critical hope, power, and social positioning. This finding illustrates Duncan-Andrade's (2009) definition of critical hope as audacious, "False hope would have us believe in individualized notions of success and suffering, but audacious hope demands that we reconnect to the collective by struggling alongside one another, sharing in the victories *and* the pain" (p. 190). In this sense, the fluid exchange of critical hope, or aspirational capital, between undocumented students and communities (i.e., collective reciprocity) serves as the lifeblood of individual and collective resistance and resilience—the source of community cultural wealth, collective power and agency.

DISCUSSION

Participants "tried to act as though they were who they said they were" by establishing relational/positional identities and by creating spaces of authoring through improvisational activity. By studying hard, following normative codes of conduct, and acting as good cultural citizens of the United States, participants illustrated the ways in which their own behaviors were indexical of claims to social relationships with others in the context of power, deference, social affiliation, and structures of the lived world. In each of their interactions, participants, consciously or subconsciously, calibrated the level of risk associated with how their position as an undocumented student related to others. When the level of risk was identified, participants mediated through the ways he/she felt comfortable or constrained, then acted accordingly.

While participants exerted agency on various levels and in various ways through improvisational activity, it was always within hegemonic norms and structures (the state) and within their socially constructed and scripted social position ("illegal alien")—undocumented student as a monolith: the deviant, uneducated, incompetent, and unwelcome immigrant. Within the confines of their undocumented status, participants engaged in an ongoing, albeit silent, inner dialogue where identities were produced, changed, and ever forming. As Luz astutely notes:

> But to continue I also depend on myself and on a lot of people even though these people are sometimes supportive and sometimes not. And so yeah, I like school. Doing well in school, I have control over something. I feel like I have control over my life. Generally, I feel like I don't have a lot of control over what happens to me. (LUZ)

In other words, their identities could only be produced and exist within individual moments, partially self-orchestrated but also bound by legal, social, and educational realities, the very aspects utilized to devise such an identity. Participants *played* within these realities, manifesting imaginary scenarios such as hyperdocumenting as a way to gain citizenship, even though such action would, in fact, not lead to such an outcome.

Without this capacity to imagine other options, there was little hope or incentive for any sense of agency—their actions were the only modicum that made any iteration of self-direction possible. The *space of authoring* that participants carved for themselves, unlike the realities of being an undocumented student, was not limited by draconian legislation or rigid rules. Instead, the space of authoring provided a continuous activity unable to be finalized or captured. Indeed, participants would evolve, change, and adapt to the various circumstances around them, authoring themselves as necessary. They maneuvered as best they could amidst social and cultural impositions. This authoring represented critical hope in action through the use of community cultural wealth. Critical hope manifested itself in the participants' strategic and organic fashioning of their identities, establishing a foundation for continuing to move forward and push back against the seemingly devastating options before them. They were unwilling to give up and leveraged their community cultural wealth as tools to keep critical hope alive.

It is from positional/relational identities, within spaces of authoring and play, and through improvisational activity that the participants' figured worlds were continuously imagined, enacted, and evolved. These figured worlds are metanarratives that will continue to develop over time and history resting on the collective "as if" realm. By imagining "as if" they will eventually become citizens, undocumented student figured worlds supply the contexts of meaning and solace for the participants' daily lived experiences and unknown futures. These figured worlds are both imagined and lived realities, rooted in the essential and continuous human experience—the development of identity, or personhood. By continually figuring their worlds, participants utilized defiance and collective power as the primary mechanisms of agency in and liberation from reproduced and imposed social landscapes. By continually figuring their worlds, participants utilized defiance and collective power as the primary mechanisms of agency in and liberation from reproduced and imposed social landscapes. Challenge was brought to the traditional US educational system that denied participants' access to the knowledge, skills, and resources needed for their matriculation, supports often denied to them as a result of their undocumented status. Through the creation of underground systems of support, participants exchanged information with other undocumented students, creating new pathways to success and accomplishing an important end. In pursuit of the American Dream via hyperdocumentation, redefinition of participants' figured worlds offered hope that their striving was not an act of futility.

While there are current political limits to undocumented students' abilities to self-advocate, many maintain critical hope as they uphold exemplary cultural citizenship even in the face of seemingly impossible odds. This study revealed the dynamic nature of this delicate dance of managing, cultivating, and enacting agency while entrenched in a process of interpreting, integrating, internalizing, and interjecting themselves as worthy objects within competing worlds of hope and despair. Undocumented students in this study showed that even from within their socially constructed and scripted social positions, they actively participated in different cultural worlds. By figuring their worlds and leveraging community cultural wealth (Yosso 2005), they created a fund of critical hope and resilience in their quest to achieve the mythological American Dream.

CONCLUSION

Undocumented students in this study illustrated their strategic use of community cultural wealth to pursue dreams that challenged everything that pointed to the contrary. Amidst the reality of not having any viable path to citizenship, these students produced identities where they could imagine "as if" figured worlds where their hyperdocumentation could increase their chances of acquiring official *papeles*, papers. Indeed, it is precisely this possibility that kept them motivated in their daily struggles. They told themselves: I know there is hope; I know my efforts are worthwhile; I know things will change. Without these beliefs, the participants were left with an impossible alternative: capitulating to legal discrimination and drowning in despair.

In many ways, we, as educators, also have a choice to make with regard to our beliefs about undocumented students. Will we believe and join in the struggle of critical hope along with our undocumented students? Or, will we succumb to the alternative? Educators are in a unique position to encourage or discourage; listen or ignore; and support or dismiss these students. The undocumented students in this study have modeled acts of resistance that have proved agentic even in the midst of potential hopelessness. How are we, as educators, improvising in our daily work to enact agency on behalf of undocumented students? How are we serving as sources of community cultural wealth for the students we work with? How can we become knowledgeable mentors and sources of support in their journeys? Most importantly, how do we ensure that we are promoting these students' sense of agency while taking responsibility for keeping ourselves well informed of the most current legal and social happenings with regard to immigration policy? Certainly, while it is valuable to commiserate in the struggles of undocumented students, it is equally valuable to construct paths of critical hope for our students. There is a danger in focusing on the obstacles rather than highlighting the powerful capital that undocumented students actually possess. The danger lies in seeing these young people through a deficit perspective rather than a strengths-based one and in that process paving a path of despair. By focusing on how individuals and collectives actively figure themselves and their worlds, we, as critical researchers and educators, can begin to also call attention to how students engage in persistence and resistance.

LIMITATIONS

While this study yielded findings that helped us identify critical themes in the context of identity, education, and agency, it was also limited in participant pool, scope, and location. The participant pool was not limited to a specific area; however, most participants lived in the same city, albeit in distinctively different neighborhoods. The term Latinx, a gender-neutral demographic category, was used as the referent for participants in this study. This term is inclusive of any person of Latin American origin or descent. Participants in this study were exclusively Latinx and therefore do not represent the true and often hidden diversity of undocumented students (Gonzales 2009). Therefore, this study is not intended to make generalizations about undocumented students. Because the number of participants was relatively small (n = 18), the study captured a non-specific group of undocumented students' experiences and their interactions with educators. Rather than make large claims about undocumented students, we used these individual experiences, as well as commonalities among them, as a launching point into a much larger, complex, and nuanced conversation about the role of identity, education, and agency for undocumented students.

NOTES

1. We intentionally leverage the term "Latinx" as a gender-neutral demographic category that includes any person of Latin American origin or descent. As Baez notes, "La flexión de género en "x" apunta a contrastar críticamente el protocolo hegemónico de la construcción masculina del sujeto universal. No es la mera inclusión -políticamente correcta- de "ellos y ellas", sino una crítica al sentido distribucionista y prescriptivo de lo masculino y lo femenino en el uso hegemónico y habitual de la gramática castellana para referirse a lxs sujetxs. La incomodidad que genera la "x" en la lectura y la pronunciación puede parangonarse con la incomodidad que sienten aquellxs que no se sienten -parcial o totalmente- representadxs/interpeladxs ni por el 'ellos' ni por el 'ellas'" (p. 2). English translation: The gender bending in "x" aims to critically contrast the hegemonic protocol in the male construction of the universal subject. It is not the mere inclusion - politically correct- of they (him) (male) and they (her) (female) but a critique of the distributive and prescriptive sense of the male and the female in the hegemonic and habitual use of the Spanish Grammar in reference to the subjects. The uncomfortable feeling that the "x" creates in the reading and the pronunciation can be compared with the uncomfortable feeling of those who do not feel - partially or totally- represented neither like they (male) or they (female).

REFERENCES

Abes, E. S. (2009). Theoretical borderlands: Using multiple theoretical perspectives to challenge inequitable power structures in student development theory. *Journal of College Student Leadership Development, 50*(2), 141–156.

Abrego, L. (2006). 'I can't go to college because I don't have papers': Incorporation patterns of Latino undocumented youth. *Latino Studies, 4*(3), 212–231.

Abrego, L. (2008). Legitimacy, social identity, and the mobilization of law: The effects of Assembly Bill 540 on undocumented students in California. *Law & Social Inquiry, 33*(3), 709–734.

Abrego, L. (2011). Legal consciousness of undocumented Latinos: Fear and stigma as barriers to claims making for first and 1.5 generation immigrants. *Law & Society Review, 45*(2), 337–369.

Abrego, L. (2014). *Sacrificing families: Navigating laws, labor, and love across borders.* Stanford: Stanford University Press.

Abrego, L., & Gonzales, R. (2010). Blocked paths, uncertain futures: The postsecondary education and labor market prospects of undocumented Latino youth. *Journal of Education for Students Placed at Risk, 15*(1–2), 144–157.

Adams, J. T. (1931). *The epic of America.* Boston: Little, Brown, & Company.

Anzaldúa, G. (1987). *Borderlands: La frontera.* Berkeley: Aunt Lute Books.

Arriaga, B. (2012). '67 sueños': Inspiring a movement for undocumented voices to be heard. *Journal of the Association of Mexican American Educators, 6*(1), 71–76.

Bagley, C., & Castro-Salazar, R. (2012). Critical arts-based research in education: Performing undocumented historias. *British Educational Research Journal, 38*(2), 239–260.

Bernal, D. D. (1997). *Chicana school resistance and grassroots leadership: Providing an alternative history of the 1968 East Los Angeles blowouts* (Doctoral dissertation).

Bernal, D. D. (1998). Using a Chicana feminist epistemology in educational research. *Harvard Educational Review, 68*(4), 555–583.

Bernal, D. D. (2002). Critical race theory, Latino critical theory, and critical raced-gendered epistemologies: Recognizing students of color as holders and creators of knowledge. *Qualitative Inquiry, 8*(1), 105–126.

Bourdieu, P. (1986). The forms of capital. In J. G. Richardson (Ed.), *Handbook of theory and research for the sociology of education* (pp. 241–258). New York: Greenwood.

Bozick, R., & Miller, T. (2014). In-state college tuition policies for undocumented immigrants: Implications for high school enrollment among non-citizen Mexican youth. *Population Research & Policy Review, 33*(1), 13–30. https://doi.org/10.1007/s11113-013-9307-4.

Burkhardt, J. C., Ortega, N., Vidal-Rodriguez, A., Frye, J. R., Nellum, C. J., Reyes, K. A., Hussain, O., Badke, L. K., & Hernandez, J. (2012). *Reconciling federal, state, and institutional policies determining educational access for undocumented students: Implications for professional practice.* Ann Arbor: National Forum on Higher Education for the Public Good.

Castro-Salazar, R., & Bagley, C. (2010). 'Ni de aquí ni from there.' Navigating between contexts: Counter-narratives of undocumented Mexican students in the United States. *Race Ethnicity and Education, 13*(1), 23–40.

Cervantes-Soon, C. G. (2012). *Testimonios* of life and learning in the borderlands: Subaltern Juárez girls speak. *Equity & Excellence in Education, 45*(3), 373–391.

Chang, A. (2011). Undocumented to hyperdocumented: A jornada of protection, papers and PhD status. *Harvard Educational Review, 81*(3), 508–520.

Chang, A., Torrez, M., Ferguson, K., & Sagar, A. (2017). Figured worlds & American dreams: An exploration of agency and identity among Latinx undocumented students. *Urban Review*. https://doi.org/10.1007/s11256-017-0397-x.

Chávez, M. L., Soriano, M., & Olivérez, P. (2007). Undocumented students' access to college: The American dream denied. *Latino Studies, 5*, 254–263. https://doi.org/10.1057/pal- grave.lst.8600255.

Chen, E. C., Budianto, L., & Wong, K. (2010). Professional school counselors as social justice advocates for undocumented immigrant students in group work. *Journal for Specialists in Group Work, 35*(3), 255–261.

Contreras, F. (2009). Sin papeles y rompiendo barreras: Latino students and the challenges of persisting in college. *Harvard Educational Review, 79*(4), 610–632.

Coutin, S. B. (2003). Borderlands, illegality and the spaces of non-existence. In R. Perry & B. Maurer (Eds.), *Globalization and governmentalities* (pp. 171–202). Minneapolis: University of Minnesota Press.

Coutin, S. B. (2005). Contesting criminality: Illegal immigration and the spatialization of legality. *Theoretical Criminology, 9*(1), 5–33.

Coutin, S. B. (2010). Exiled by law: Deportation and the inviability of life. In N. De Genova & N. Peutz (Eds.), *The deportation regime: Sovereignty, space, and the freedom of movement*. Durham: Duke University Press.

Coutin, S. B. (2011a). The rights of non-citizens in the United States. *Annual Review of Law & Social Science, 7*, 289–308.

Coutin, S. B. (2011b). Legal exclusion and dislocated subjectivities: The deportation of Salvadoran youth from the United States. In V. J. Squire (Ed.), *The contested politics of mobility: Borderzones and irregularity* (pp. 169–183). London: Routledge.

Coutin, S. B. (2013). In the breach: Citizenship and its approximations. *Indiana Journal of Global Legal Studies, 20*(1), 109–140.

Covarrubias, A., & Lara, A. (2014). The undocumented (im)migrant educational pipeline: The influence of citizenship status on educational attainment for people of Mexican origin. *Urban Education, 49*(1), 75–110.

Crenshaw, K. (1989). Demarginalizing the intersection of race and sex: A black feminist critique of antidiscrimination doctrine, feminist theory and antiracist politics. *University of Chicago Legal Forum, 140*, 139–167.

Crenshaw, K. (1991). Mapping the margins: Intersectionality, identity politics, and violence against women of color. *Stanford Law Review, 43*(6), 1241–1299.

De Genova, N. P. (2002). Migrant 'illegality' and deportability in everyday life. *Annual Review of Anthropology, 31,* 419–437.

De Genova, N. (2005). *Working the boundaries: Race, space, and "illegality" in Mexican Chicago.* Durham: Duke University Press.

De Genova, N. (Ed.). (2006). *Racial transformations: Latinos and Asians remaking the United States.* Durham: Duke University Press.

De Genova, N., & Peutz, N. (Eds.). (2010). The deportation regime: Sovereignty, space, and the freedom of movement. Durham, NC: Duke University Press.

De Genova, N., & Ramos-Zayas, A. Y. (2003). Latino crossings: Mexicans, Puerto Ricans, and the politics of race and citizenship. New York, NY: Routledge.

Diaz-Strong, D., Gomez, C., Luna-Duarte, M. E., & Meiners, E. R. (2011). Purged: Undocumented students, financial aid policies, and access to higher education. *Journal of Hispanic Higher Education, 10*(2), 107–119.

Dougherty, K. J., Nienhusser, H. K., & Vega, B. (2010). Undocumented immigrants and state higher education policy: The politics of in-state tuition eligibility in Texas and Arizona. *Review of Higher Education, 34*(1), 123–173.

Dozier, S. B. (2001). Undocumented and documented international students: A comparative study of their academic performance. *Community College Review, 29*(2), 43–53. https://doi.org/10.1177/009155210102900204.

Duncan-Andrade, J. M. R. (2009). Note to educators: Hope required when growing roses in concrete. *Harvard Educational Review, 79*(2), 181–194.

Ellis, L. M., & Chen, E. C. (2013). Negotiating identity development among undocumented immigrant college students: A grounded theory study. *Journal of Counseling Psychology, 60*(2), 251–264.

Enriquez, L. E. (2011). "Because we feel the pressure and we also feel the support": Examining the educational success of undocumented immigrant Latina/o students. *Harvard Educational Review, 81*(3), 476–500.

Enriquez, L. E. (2014). "Undocumented and citizen students unite": Building a cross-status coalition through shared ideology. *Social Problems, 61*(2), 155–174. https://doi.org/10.1525/sp.2014.12032.

Flores, S. (2010). State dream acts: The effect of in-state resident tuition policies and undocumented Latino students. *Review of Higher Education, 38*(1), 239–283.

Flores, S. M., & Horn, C. L. (2009). College persistence among undocumented students at a selective public university: A quantitative case study analysis. *Journal of College Student Retention: Research, Theory and Practice, 11*(1), 57–76.

Fontana, A., & Frey, J. H. (2000). The interview—From structured questions to negotiated text. In N. Denzin & Y. Lincoln (Eds.), *Handbook of qualitative research.* Thousand Oaks: Sage.

Freire, P. (1970). *Pedagogy of the oppressed* (M. B. Ramos, Trans.). New York: Continuum.

Freire, P. (1973). *Education for critical consciousness* (Vol. 1). New York: Bloomsbury Publishing.

Galindo, R. (2011). Embodying the gap between national inclusion and exclusion: The congressional testimony of three undocumented students. *Harvard Latino Law Review, 14,* 377–395.

Galindo, R. (2012). Undocumented & unafraid: The DREAM Act 5 and the public disclosure of undocumented status as a political act. *Urban Review: Issues and Ideas in Public Education, 44*(5), 589–611.

Garcia, L. D., & Tierney, W. G. (2011). Undocumented immigrants in higher education: A preliminary analysis. *Teachers College Record, 113*(12), 2739–2776.

Gilbert, M. J. (1982). *Cultural determinants in alcohol help seeking.* Proposal to the National Institute of Alcohol and Alcohol Abuse, Research Fellowship Program.

Giroux, H. A. (1983). *Theory and resistance in education: A pedagogy for the opposition.* South Hadley: Bergin & Garvey.

Glenn, E. (2011). Constructing citizenship: Exclusion, subordination, and resistance. *American Sociological Review, 76*(1), 1–24.

Gonzales, R. G. (2008). Left out but not shut down: Political activism and the undocumented student movement. *Northwestern Journal of Law and Social Policy, 3*(2), 219–239.

Gonzales, R. (2009). Special report: Young lives on hold: The college dreams of undocumented students. *The College Board,* 1–27.

Gonzales, R. G. (2010). On the wrong side of the tracks: Understanding the effects of school structure and social capital in the educational pursuits of undocumented immigrant students. *Peabody Journal of Education, 85*(4), 46.

Gonzales, R. G. (2011). Learning to be illegal undocumented youth and shifting legal contexts in the transition to adulthood. *American Sociological Review, 76*(4), 602–619.

Hernandez, I., Mendoza, F., Lio, M., Latthi, J., & Eusebio, C. (2011). Things I'll never say: Stories of growing up undocumented in the United States. *Harvard Educational Review, 81*(3), 500–508.

Hochschild, J. L. (1995). *Facing up the American dream: Race, class, and the soul of the nation.* Princeton: Princeton University Press.

Holland, D., Lachicotte, W., Skinner, D., & Cain, C. (1998). *Agency and identity in cultural worlds.* Cambridge, MA: Harvard University Press.

Huber, L. P. (2010). Using Latina/o critical race theory (LatCrit) and racist nativism to explore intersectionality in the educational experiences of undocumented Chicana college students. *Educational Foundations, 24*(1–2), 77–96.

Huber, L. P., & Malagon, M. C. (2007). Silenced struggles: The experiences of Latina and Latino undocumented college students in California. *The Nevada Journal, 7,* 841–861.

Huber, L. P., Malagon, M. C., & Solorzano, D. G. (2009). *Struggling for opportunity: Undocumented AB 540 students in the Latina/o education pipeline* (CSRC research report no. 13). UCLA Chicano Studies Research Center.

Jacobo, R., & Ochoa, A. M. (2011). Examining the experiences of undocumented college students: Walking the known and unknown lived spaces. *Journal of the Association of Mexican American Educators, 5*(1), 22–30.

Kincheloe, J. L., & McLaren, P. (2005). Rethinking critical theory and qualitative research. In N. K. Denzin & Y. S. Lincoln (Eds.), *The Sage handbook of qualitative research* (pp. 303–342). Thousand Oaks: Sage.

King, K. A., & Punti, G. (2012). On the margins: Undocumented students' narrated experiences of (il)legality. *Linguistics and Education: An International Research Journal, 23*(3), 235–249.

Lincoln, Y., & Guba, E. G. (1985). *Naturalistic inquiry*. Beverly Hills: Sage.

Lopez, J. (2010). *Undocumented students and the policies of wasted potential*. El Paso: LFB Scholarly Publishing.

Madison, D. S. (2005). *Critical ethnography: Method, ethics and performance*. Thousand Oaks: Sage.

McLaren, P. (1993). Multiculturalism and the postmodern critique: Towards a pedagogy of resistance and transformation. *Cultural Studies, 7*(1), 118–146.

Menjívar, C., & Abrego, L. (2009). Parents and children across borders: Legal instability and intergenerational relations in Guatemalan and Salvadoran families. In N. Foner (Ed.), *Across generations: Immigrant families in America* (pp. 160–189). New York: New York University Press.

Muñoz, S. M. (2015). *Identity, social activism, and the pursuit of higher education: The journey stories of undocumented and unafraid community activists*. New York: Peter Lang.

Muñoz, S. M., & Maldonado, M. M. (2012). Counterstories of college persistence by undocumented Mexicana students: Navigating race, class, gender, and legal status. *International Journal of Qualitative Studies in Education, 25*(3), 293–315.

Negrón-Gonzales, G. (2014). Undocumented, unafraid and unapologetic: Re-articulatory practices and migrant youth "illegality". *Latino Studies, 12*(2), 259–278.

Nguyen, D. K., & Serna, G. R. (2014). Access or barrier? Tuition and fee legislation for undocumented students across the States. *Clearing House, 87*(3), 124–129. https://doi.org/10.1080/00098655.2014.891895.

Nicholls, W. (2013). *The DREAMers: How the undocumented youth movement transformed the immigrant rights debate*. Palo Alto: Stanford University Press.

Nienhusser, H. K. (2014). Role of community colleges in the implementation of postsecondary education enrollment policies for undocumented students. *Community College Review, 42*(1), 3–22. https://doi.org/10.1177/0091552113509837.

Olivas, M. A. (2012). *No undocumented child left behind: Plyler v. Doe and the education of undocumented schoolchildren*. New York: New York University Press.

Orner, P. (2008). *Underground America: Narratives of undocumented lives*. San Francisco: McSweeney's.

Ortiz, A. M., & Hinojosa, A. (2010). Tenuous options: The career development process for undocumented students. *New Directions for Student Services, 131,* 53–65.

Passel, J. S., & Cohn, D. (2016, September). *Unauthorized immigrant population stable for half a decade*. Washington, DC: Pew Research Center. Retrieved from http://www.pewresearch.org/fact-tank/2016/09/21/unauthorized-immigrant-population-stable-for-half-a-decade/

Patel, L. (2013). *Youth held at the border: Immigration, education and the politics of inclusion*. New York: Teachers College Press.

Patton, M. Q. (1990). *Qualitative evaluation and research methods*. Newbury Park: Sage.

Pérez, W. (2009). *We are Americans*. Sterling: Stylus.

Pérez, P. A. (2010a). College choice process of Latino undocumented students: Implications for recruitment and retention. *Journal of College Admission, 206,* 21–25.

Pérez, W. (2010b). Higher education access for undocumented students: Recommendations for counseling professionals. *Journal of College Admission, 206,* 32–35.

Pérez, W. (2012). *Americans by heart: Undocumented Latino students and the promise of higher education*. New York: Teachers College Press.

Pérez, W., & Cortés, R. D. (2011). *Undocumented Latino college students: Their socioemotional and academic experiences*. El Paso: LFB Scholarly Pub. LLC.

Pérez, P. A., & Rodriguez, J. L. (2011). Access and opportunity for Latina/o undocumented college students: Familial and institutional support factors. *Journal of the Association of Mexican American Educators, 5*(1), 14–21.

Pérez, W., Espinoza, R., Ramos, K., Coronado, H. M., & Cortes, R. (2009). Academic resilience among undocumented Latino students. *Hispanic Journal of Behavioral Sciences, 31*(2), 149–181.

Rincon, A. (2010). !Si se puede!: Undocumented immigrants' struggle for education and their right to stay. *Journal of College Admission, 206,* 13–18.

Rodriguez, G. M., & Cruz, L. (2009). The transition to college of English learner and undocumented immigrant students: Resource and policy implications. *Teachers College Record, 111*(10), 2385–2418.

Román, E. (2013). *Those damned immigrants: America's hysteria over undocumented immigration*. New York: New York University Press.

Ryscavage, R., & Canaris, M. M. (2013). Undocumented students ask Jesuit higher ed: "Just us" or justice? *New England Journal of Higher Education*. Retrieved from: http://www.nebhe.org/thejournal/undocumented-students-ask-jesuit-higher-education-just-us-or-justice/

Solórzano, D. G., & Bernal, D. D. (2001). Examining transformational resistance through a critical race and LatCrit theory framework: Chicana and Chicano students in an urban context. *Urban Education, 36*(3), 308–342.

Stanton-Salazar, R. (2001). *Manufacturing hope and despair: The school and kin support networks of U.S. Mexican youth.* New York: Teachers College Press.

Storlie, C. A., & Jach, E. A. (2012). Social justice collaboration in schools: A model for working with undocumented Latino students. *Journal for Social Action in Counseling & Psychology, 4*(2), 99–116.

Suárez-Orozco, C., Suárez-Orozco, M. M., & Todorova, I. (2010). *Learning a new land: Immigrant students in American society.* Cambridge, MA: Belknap Press of Harvard University Press.

Syme, S. L. (2004). Social determinants of health: The community as empowered partner. *Preventing Chronic Disease: Public Health Research, Practice, and Policy, 1*(1), 1–4.

Torres, R., & Wicks-Asbun, M. (2014). Undocumented students' narratives of liminal citizenship: High aspirations, exclusion, and "in-between" identities. *Professional Geographer, 66*(2), 195–204. https://doi.org/10.1080/00330124.2012.735936.

Vargas, E. D. (2011). In-state tuition policies for undocumented youth. *Harvard Journal of Hispanic Policy, 23*, 43–58.

Viramontez Anguiano, R. P., & Lopez, A. (2012). "El miedo y el hambre": Understanding the familial, social, and educational realities of undocumented Latino families in North Central Indiana. *Journal of Family Social Work, 15*(4), 321–336.

West, C. (2004). The impossible will take a little while. In P. Rogat (Ed.), *The impossible will take a little while: A citizen's guide to hope in a time of fear* (pp. 293–297). New York: Basic Books.

West, C. (2008). *Hope on a tightrope.* New York: Smiley Books.

Yosso, T. J. (2005). Whose culture has capital? A critical race theory discussion of community cultural wealth. *Race, Ethnicity, and Education, 8*(1), 69–91.

CHAPTER 5

Doing Good and Doing Damage: Educators' Impact on Undocumented Latinx Students' Lives

The Trump administration's anti-immigrant actions have heightened the urgency to address issues that undocumented people face; this is especially true for undocumented Latinx students. Latinx students comprise the majority of undocumented immigrants within US K-16 educational institutions and are therefore disproportionately impacted by such policies. While undocumented students remain vulnerable to the hostile political climate and simultaneously self-empowered through their own activism, educators have a particularly poignant role in impacting undocumented students' lives. In this chapter, we draw from the perspectives of undocumented students to examine how educators impact undocumented Latinx lives for better or for worse. Drawing on a qualitative study of 18 undocumented students, we focus on undocumented Latinx students' perceptions of educators' everyday interactions with them and use Valenzuela's (1999) notions of educación and authentic caring to analyze how students make meaning of them. Based on our findings, we stress the significance of interactions that do good and others that do damage and suggest that educators can powerfully influence the lives of undocumented youth through small, even momentary interactions.

This article was originally co-authored by Aurora Chang and Ingrid Colon and submitted for review in 2017.

© The Author(s) 2018
A. Chang, *The Struggles of Identity, Education, and Agency in the Lives of Undocumented Students*, https://doi.org/10.1007/978-3-319-64614-5_5

A growing and relatively robust research base on DREAMers and DACAmented students as undergraduates, graduate students, and those entering the workforce has recently emerged. Most of the research resides in the field of higher education and less in K-12 settings with a particular focus on policy-level issues and individual student narratives. However, little research has exclusively focused on what educators, across all levels and roles, can do and have done to both support and damage undocumented students. Studying the impact of educators' actions and omissions from the vantage point of undocumented students is critical to informing current practices, behaviors, and interventions. This study attempts to begin a conversation around the role of educators in undocumented students' lives by asking: How do undocumented students perceive their everyday interactions with educators? Of these interactions, which ones do students identify as "doing good" and "doing damage"? In this chapter, we argue, through the words of our undocumented participants, that individual educators have the power to "do good" or "do damage" in the lives of undocumented youth. We analyze, discuss, and present implications about the impact of educators on undocumented students, noting that the actions and omissions of individual educators can have lasting effects on their lives. Among our participants, we found "children who have been raised to dream, yet are cut off from the very mechanisms that allow them to achieve their dreams" (Gonzales 2009, p. 6); their dreams are tempered and even, squashed by limited educational opportunities, low academic expectations, fear of deportation, inability to acquire employment, and mental health challenges associated with the stress of being undocumented. In the midst of such adversity, our participants pointed to human mechanisms that can serve as gateways or gatekeepers for the futures of undocumented students—those human mechanisms are educators. In this chapter, we focus on educators' influence on the lives of undocumented students by, first, situating our topic within the extant research about undocumented students, presenting our theoretical framework, outlining the study's methodology, presenting three major findings, and ending with a discussion and implications.

EXISTING RESEARCH ABOUT UNDOCUMENTED STUDENTS

The extant literature around education and undocumented Latinx students addresses a range of issues. Here, we present an overview of these issues by categorizing them into themes, followed by the respective pertinent scholarship. We present a comprehensive, though not exhaustive, context in which to situate our own study.

Over the past ten years, there has been a spike in research around undocumented students and specifically related to the DREAM Act, DREAMers, DACA, and DACAmented students. Accordingly, studies have primarily focused on undergraduate undocumented students and issues within higher education contexts, including in-state tuition policies (Bozick and Miller 2014; Dougherty et al. 2010; Flores 2010; Nguyen and Serna 2014; Vargas 2011) and access to higher education (Burkhardt et al. 2012; Chávez et al. 2007; Diaz-Strong et al. 2011; Garcia and Tierney 2011; Gonzales 2009; Huber et al. 2009; Pérez and Rodriguez 2011). Related to this focus, studies have also examined academic performance and issues of recruiting, admitting, and retaining undocumented students (Abrego 2006; Enriquez 2011; Gonzales 2010; Pérez 2010a, b; Pérez and Rodriguez 2011; Rincon 2010; Ryscavage and Canaris 2013). Undocumented students' successful navigation of academia has also been of particular interest (Chang 2016; Contreras 2009; Dozier 2001; Flores and Horn 2009; Garcia and Tierney 2011; Pérez et al. 2009). Finally, within the field of higher education, studies have looked at the poignant issue of undocumented students' post-secondary paths/careers/employment (lack of) options (Abrego and Gonzales 2010; Jacobo and Ochoa 2011; López 2010; Ortiz and Hinojosa 2010; Rodriguez and Cruz 2009).

Within K-12, research has emerged about particularly academically successful undocumented students (Covarrubias and Lara 2014; Enriquez 2011; Gonzales 2010; Pérez et al. 2009; Lopez 2010; Viramontez Anguiano and Lopez 2012). Other provocative pieces of research have honed in on the legal impacts, challenges, and implications of undocumented status (Abrego 2006, 2008, 2011; Menjívar and Abrego 2009; Coutin 2010, 2011a, b; Olivas 2012; Román 2013).

Studies have also relied on undocumented narratives and *testimonios* by people of various ages, including children and adolescents (King and Punti 2012; Patel 2013), young adults (Arriaga 2012; Castro-Salazar and Bagley 2010; Galindo 2011, 2012; Hernandez et al. 2011; Huber and Malagon 2007; Pérez-Huber 2010; Torres and Wicks-Asbun 2014), and college students/adults (Bagley and Castro-Salazar 2012; Chang 2011; Jacobo and Ochoa 2011; Orner 2008; Pérez 2009). Program case studies in both K-12 (Chen et al. 2010; Rodriguez and Cruz 2009; Storlie and Jach 2012) and higher education (Bagley and Castro-Salazar 2012; Enriquez 2014; Nienhusser 2014) have also served as methodological approaches to understanding the educational experiences of undocumented students.

Additionally, some scholars have theorized around undocumented experiences as they relate to hyperdocumentation (Chang 2011), deportability in everyday life (De Genova 2002), identity development (Chang et al. 2017; Ellis and Chen 2013), social activism (Muñoz 2015), constructing citizenship (Coutin 2010, 2013; Glenn 2011), race, spatialization, borderlands, and "illegality" (Coutin 2003, 2005; De Genova 2005, 2006; De Genova and Peutz 2010; De Genova and Ramos-Zayas 2003) and methodological ethics (Chang 2015).

So while substantive research, as evidenced from the literature review above and from forerunners in this field as we will exemplify below, has explored the complex issues around undocumented students' educational paths, studies that primarily focus on educators' interventions and practices are few or tangentially addressed. In their comprehensive overview of the possibilities and challenges that immigrant children face in K-12 public schools and the policies necessary for them to become successful students and people, Suárez-Orozco et al. (2010) have laid the foundation for the eminent work awaiting scholars of immigrant students and the "less than optimal" (p. 88) conditions that immigrant students face. Pérez's (2009, 2012) and Roberto Gonzales's (2009) work on undocumented Latinx students and higher education has been groundbreaking in capturing the "legal paradox" (Gonzales 2009, p. 25) and educational obstacles they face due to their undocumented status. However, our study hopes to fill a gap in the current research by specifically focusing on undocumented Latinx students' perceptions of their everyday interactions with educators

Theoretical Framework: Educación and Authentic Caring

We utilize Valenzuela's (1999) notions of educación and authentic caring as our theoretical framework. Valenzuela's (1999) work with Mexican students at Seguín High School illustrates the critical importance of the authentic caring relationship between students and teachers—one that is grounded in Latinx cultural understandings of educación. Valenzuela defines educación as "the family's role of inculcating in children a sense of moral, social, and personal responsibility and... a competence in the social world, wherein one respects the dignity and individuality of others" (p. 23). De Jesús and Antrop-González (2006) and Antrop-González and De Jesús (2006) add to this notion by including cultural constructs such as personalismo (characterized as high-quality interpersonal relationships), and the Puerto Rican notion of hard caring (the high expectation of academic excellence, coupled with follow-through and consequences for low performance).

According to Valenzuela (1999), authentic caring "emphasizes relations of reciprocity between teachers and students" (p. 61). In fact, she claims that it is the basis for all learning, noting that "authentically caring teachers are seized by their students and energy flows toward their projects and needs" (p. 61). Perhaps most important to this study is the idea that "despite perceiving themselves as caring, many teachers unconsciously communicate a different message" (pp. 63–64)—it is through this lens that we approach this research. Educators, regardless of intent, can "do good" and "do harm" to undocumented students. Rather than place judgment on educators, we seek to present examples that illustrate the impact of educators' actions on undocumented students so as to provide a launching point for discussion and self-reflection that can lead to increased pedagogical self-awareness.

METHODOLOGY

Procedure

This chapter draws from a qualitative study of 18 diverse Latinx individuals, ages 18 and above, who identified as undocumented or once undocumented students (see Table 5.1) to address the following research question: How do undocumented students perceive their everyday interactions with educators? And, of these interactions, which ones do students identify as "doing good" and "doing damage"? Participants were recruited via e-mail invitation and through the snowball sampling method (Patton 1990), and data was collected through semi-structured interviews (Fontana and Frey 2000). Because of the vulnerable legal status of this population, we paid particular attention to confidentiality, paying special care to the importance of rapport, a component that is "essential in helping to create for the participant the feeling of being respected and of being genuinely heard" (Madison 2005, p. 31). While we were interested in the findings of this research, we understood that our primary responsibility was to those studied. We conducted open-ended interviews, each lasting between 45 and 90 minutes. All interviews were digitally audio-recorded with participant permission, and pseudonyms were used in documenting the data.

Table 5.1 Participant information

	Pseudonym	Sex	Age	Country of birth	Arrived to the United States	Occupation	Current residence	Immigration status
1	Luz	F	21	Mexico	4 years old	College student	Chicago, IL	DACAmented
2	Aura	F	23	Mexico	3 months old	Graduate student/waitress	Chicago, IL	Undocumented
3	Yaelisa	F	22	Mexico	10 years old	Graduate student/travel agent	Chicago, IL	DACAmented
4	Nina	F	22	Mexico	2 years old	College student	Beloit, WI	DACAmented
5	Daniela	F	24	Mexico	9 months old	Stay-at-home mom	Chicago, IL	Undocumented
6	Lydia	F	26	Mexico	12 years old	Graduate student	Chicago, IL	DACAmented
7	Esperanza	F	19	Mexico	8 years old	College student	Chicago, IL	DACAmented
8	Alejandro	M	24	Mexico	14 years old	Graduate student/nonprofit work	Ann Arbor, MI	DACAmented
9	Moises	M	26	Mexico	11 years old	Military	Austin, TX	DACAmented
10	Flor	F	23	Mexico	9 years old	Graduate student/research assistant	Chicago, IL	DACAmented
11	Katerina	F	21	Nicaragua	5 years old	Bilingual advocate for sexual assault	Madison, WI	DACAmented
12	Enrique	M	23	Mexico	13 years old	College student	Chicago, IL	DACAmented
13	Laura	F	22	Mexico	5 years old	College student/barista	Petaluma, CA	DACAmented
14	Maria	F	21	Mexico	5 years old	College student	Laramie, WY	DACAmented
15	Pepe	M	25	Mexico	6 years old	College student	Laramie, WY	DACAmented
16	Dolores	F	23	Mexico	4 years old	Unemployed	Chicago, IL	Citizen via marriage
17	Carlos	M	25	Mexico	1 year old	Day labor center manager	Sonoma, CA	DACAmented
18	Chavo	M	26	Guatemala	2 months old	Student affairs program coordinator	Sacramento, CA	DACAmented

While this study yielded findings that helped us identify critical educational interventions and practices that impacted undocumented Latinx students, it was also limited in participant pool, scope, and location. The participant pool was not limited to a specific area; however, most participants lived in the same city, albeit in distinctly different neighborhoods. The participants were also exclusively Latinx and therefore do not represent the true and often hidden diversity of undocumented students (Gonzales 2009). Therefore, this study is not intended to make generalizations about undocumented students, nor about educators who work with them. Because the number of participants was relatively small (n = 18), the study captured a non-specific group of undocumented students' experiences and their interactions with educators. Rather than make large claims about undocumented students, we used these individual experiences, as well as commonalities among them, as a launching point to show the potential implications that may exist for educators in supporting and/or damaging undocumented students' lives. In other words, this study provides a window into a much larger, complex, and nuanced conversation about the role of educators with undocumented students, specifically the anatomy of inequality that pervades US educational institutions. Our participants provided us with snapshots of their educational experience within a multilayered landscape of educational mire.

Data Analysis

After data was collected, the interviews were transcribed and uploaded to Crocodoc, an embedded HTML5 document viewer that allows multiple users to annotate a single document. Each interview transcript was coded by each of us using an open coding method, tracking our coding through the insertion of comments (explaining the code) directly linked to specific quotations within the transcripts. We followed inductive data analysis throughout the data-collection process (Lincoln and Guba 1985). We created codes to characterize participants' comments, reviewed each code, and compared them to make sure each was relatively unique and that they encompassed fairly heterogeneous codes. We produced a list of 88 supercodes with an average of three subcodes per supercode. Following this process, we reviewed the codes. We analyzed both commonalities and variations among the codes. Codes that related to the same content were grouped together in "provisional categories" (Lincoln and Guba 1985, p. 347) by collaboratively identifying emerging code patterns or dominant themes. The identification of emerging code patterns or dominant themes allowed us to capture central key narratives that rose to the surface. We identified specific participant quotes that illustrated this theme and, from there, discussed the meaning and implications of these quotes. After discussing the quotes with one another through the course of five one-hour meetings, we revisited the quotations to ensure that we didn't overlook any significant ones. Finally, we developed subthemes that eventually served as our findings.

FINDINGS

In this section, we report on the study's findings about undocumented Latinx students' perceptions of the role of educators in their students' lives. The findings are organized into three major themes: doing good, doing damage, and maintaining hope. We begin with the ways participants indicated that educators supported them. Then, we explore participants' recollections of how educators damaged them. Finally, we relay participants' navigation of hope amidst their unforeseeable contexts.

Doing Good

There were those educators who served as advocates and champions for our participants—doing good by them at all costs. In our study, the participants consistently stressed the importance of daily interactions among students and educators. Among the traits they considered pivotal in educators were having high expectations of them, authentically caring, connecting with their cultural background, and taking part in and becoming knowledgeable about the issues that undocumented students face. In this section, we focus on our participants' experiences with educators. For example, Enrique recommended that educators "be open and listen to their students and encourage them to seek out help." He stressed that "a lot of undocumented students don't ask for help because they are afraid or they don't feel comfortable." In contrast, Chavo remembered two teachers who not only made him feel comfortable but were equally rigorous and helpful.

> Miss Johnson actually also employed my mom as a house cleaner. I didn't have her because the year that I was supposed to have her, she took a leave. But she was the kind of teacher that was like, "If you guys need help, if you guys need to stay after school to do anything, I'm here for you guys." Then

we had Mr. Miller who within that school district was the superintendent, the principal, and the 6th grade teacher. He was like, "I have high expectations of you. I'm not letting you do that as a kind of excuse not to excel in this class and be at the same level as the rest of your peers. If you need extra help, I will help you to meet my expectations of you." He let us know.

When educators clearly went out of their way to support and maximize our participants' academic potential despite their immigration status, our participants felt authentically cared for (Valenzuela 1999). Valenzuela (1999) defines authentic caring as one that is grounded in Mexican cultural understandings of educación. In contrast to schooling, Valenzuela defines educación as, "the family's role of inculcating in children a sense of moral, social, and personal responsibility and a competence in the social world, wherein one respects the dignity and individuality of others" (23). Specifically, participants' narratives hearkened back to Duncan Andrade's (2009) notion of "all around positive harassment" (p. 8) as particularly effective, underscoring the effective act of insisting and not giving up on students to succeed in school. This persistence from educators in supporting all of their students was seen as a loving, rigorous, and playful way of showing authentic care. In direct alignment with this care, participants recalled the specific ways in which educators were involved in the local community, usually the one in which the participants lived. As Aura recalled:

My sixth grade teacher was one of the teachers that stood out to me the most. And I also had a high school teacher. They were very involved in the community and they would always give us advice because the school that I went to was, the majority were Latinos. And they wished the best for us and they'd show us so much and made us reflect a lot about where we stood in society and how we could improve, and help us with whatever needed to be addressed.

Participants referred to seeing these educators at church, being involved in social-justice protests, providing English classes to their Spanish-speaking parents, showing up at community events, and having relationships with people (in addition to students) within the community. They indicated that there was a direct relationship between educators who were active in their communities and those who were trustworthy advocates for them.

Participants also highlighted the importance of connecting with educators on a cultural level. Luz fondly remembered an educator who she closely related to:

> Yeah, my advisor, she was also one of my professors. She was the advisor to the undocumented student organization and she's an immigrant herself, I'm not sure if legally, she's very helpful in reaching new students and how to go about finding resources.

Lydia also pointed to the special impact of professors who shared an identity with her and who could specifically relate to being "subordinated within the academy":

> This generation of working class faculty professors come from backgrounds like mine. It's just nice having that understanding based on having classes with them. Getting to connect with more professors and exchange ideas with them, establishing a relationship. Talking about different opportunities with them and building those personal relationships even though they are still subordinated within the academy.

Nina recalled a classroom experience that speaks to the importance of raising conflict and difficult conversations during class:

Nina: As an undocumented student myself, I don't feel like you really know about me unless you've lived that experience. Well, when professors say you know, let me talk about immigration but we don't really talk about it. I was in an education class where it was mainly on, I forgot the actual title, but it's sort of like poverty in schools, and a lot of things that restrict students from pursuing education and it wasn't even on the syllabus to talk about immigration but then once it got brought up, it wasn't much in a way. Educators should really educate on the topic.

First Author: So, it's like superficial?

Nina: Yes, that's what I mean that's why I used the word, fake.

First Author: And do you think that's because instructors don't know how to talk about it or what do you think?

Nina: For me, yes. I won't say I totally blame them especially when they haven't lived through that, it could really be challenging but maybe you get to know actual people that have went through those experiences that you your-self have not. That way they'll know firsthand—well, not firsthand—but like really close how it impacts the stu-dents rather than just reading about it because from reading about it you can say the same thing over and over and over again. There's a lot of stories like mine and there's going to be so many stories that sound the same but every story is unique to that specific individual.

Nina later emphasized that she lacked trust in teachers who were not will-ing to talk about potentially controversial topics in the interest of keeping the class "safe." It was exactly in those instances of curricular omission or avoidance that Nina felt unsafe; she interpreted these moments as stem-ming from her teachers' discomfort or unwillingness to discuss potentially difficult topics, which in turn did not inspire confidence in the teacher's facilitation abilities, discouraging Nina from participating.

Doing Damage

Our participants vividly recalled experiences with educators who damaged them to various degrees. The kind of damage that was done ranged from the reinforcement of stereotypes, discrimination, being treated as unde-serving of education, and discouragement to pursue higher education, to being insensitive and often ignorant or forgetful about their situations as undocumented students. As Yaelisa explained when she made the transi-tion from a bilingual classroom to an English-only classroom, "I felt con-fident but also felt scared that my teacher was going to be mean to the new students who were added to the English class. It is because after my expe-rience with my fifth grade teacher, I was scared with all teachers." Her fifth-grade teacher made her feel "less than" other students because of her undocumented status and her difficulty in learning English as a second language. For Yaelisa, it took only one educator to impact the way she viewed her future teachers and education overall. Yaelisa understood that this teacher held deep-seated convictions about immigrants that carried into her interactions with students. Not surprisingly, the way educators interact with undocumented students can be explained by their own per-ceptions and beliefs that they have around immigration issues. One of our participants, Carlos, explained his context as one of the only Latina/o students going to an upper-class public school in an area of the country known for its wine production. He and his family, along with a few other immigrant families, worked for the local vineyards picking grapes, and therefore he went to school with the children of vineyard owners, CEOs, and philanthropists. Carlos recalled:

> I have wonderful memories of most of my teachers within that school. The only one that I hated, that really turned me off was a teacher that I had. Her name was Ms. Lennox (pseudonym). She just did not like me and all of my friends. She did everything in her power to make sure that we knew that she didn't like us. She had us tested for learning disabilities. She just turned me off completely from the world of math. I blame her for not being an engineer. I still think to this day that she had something against the fact that I was in school. We were given access to more resources than what we would have otherwise had if we didn't live in that rich neighborhood. So I think she was kind of like, "Oh, you guys shouldn't be here" type of thing.

Participants consistently revealed that they were aware of specific educators who made them feel as if they were undeserving of an education and were punished through low academic expectations and/or disciplinary measures such as being unfairly accused of misbehaving, being sent out of class for minor infractions, and generally being expected to fail. Understandably, participants felt discouraged and angry. Katerina, a Mexican, undocumented student, expressed her frustration with the assumptions that she felt teachers commonly made about undocumented students. She explained:

> That we aren't trying to go to college or that we're just trying to abuse the system. But I hear a lot about people thinking that we get a lot of assistance from the government or something like that and that we're not really trying hard to succeed or go to college. I don't know if they don't know, if they're not really aware that we can't get financial aid so going to college might not be a possibility. Yeah, that's something very hard.

This ignorance on the part of educators fed feelings of resentment toward undocumented students and unfairly impacted the ways in which they were treated. Interestingly, some educators' lack of information or abundance of misinformation stemmed from good intentions but resulted in poor practices. Dolores explained this conundrum when she described her experiences with a college academic advisor:

> I actually had a lot of problems with my advisor not understanding at all about my status. I remember she called me in, I think it was my sophomore year, she's like, "Okay let's talk, what's your plan for this year?" I didn't mention studying abroad so she kind of asked me, told me like, "You have so much potential but you hold yourself back—the way I see it." I guess she was trying to say that I wasn't trying hard enough, that I could be challenging myself more than just sticking around.

Her advisor had the right idea—she was trying to encourage Dolores to seize an opportunity. However, she failed to realize that Dolores couldn't study abroad; she couldn't travel because she didn't have the proper identification to get on a plane. Dolores's decision not to pursue the study-abroad opportunity had nothing to do with studying abroad per se—she would have loved to study abroad; it had everything to do with her undocumented immigration status. Indeed, her advisor's good intention to encourage Dolores lacked an integral piece of information. Rather than encourage Dolores, she made her feel that she hadn't been listened to; it was like pouring salt on a wound. As we will show in the next section, our participants were close observers of educators' behaviors and would cautiously choose those to whom they would reveal their undocumented status.

We found that undocumented students appreciated educators' efforts to assist them; however, they made a clear distinction between educators pitying them and genuinely caring. As Yaelisa noted, "Even though they made it seem like they cared and they were advocates, at the same time it made me feel like, like they just felt pity for me, and this would anger me and I didn't like that feeling." Yaelisa clearly recalled that educators felt sorry for her situation but were unable to support her in immediate, meaningful, or long-term ways. Experiences like this led participants to distrust potential educators. Enrique explained his frustration and hesitation with the emotional turmoil involved in deciding to disclose his undocumented status.

> I wouldn't say that I was afraid that I was gonna get deported or that somebody was gonna call the police on me or anything like that. It's more that I didn't want to deal with explaining the situation or things like that to anybody who's just being curious rather than actually caring.

Participants needed to be certain that the educator cared about them rather than seeing them as a novelty before they even considered coming out to them. This distrust, then, created a barrier for students to reach out to some educators because they felt they were not going to truly advocate for them or, worse, that they would inappropriately share their information. Participants pointed out that some educators had a negative impact on them simply by avoiding the issue altogether. As Alejandro explained:

> I feel like a lot of the issues right now with teachers is that they're afraid of like hurting the students, feeling in some way like they might approach them the wrong way, and sometimes they don't even do that at all. I feel like that's getting promoted in another way; that they're framing issues to undocumented students but like hey it's really sensitive. They are being told "you should probably back off and just be there in case they come to you" but there's no one offering tips on how to be proactive I think. It's just like you should sit back and if they come to you, like be nice.

Alejandro got the sense that educators were both afraid and misinformed about how to work with undocumented students. In other words, educators lacked the training and information on how they could advocate for undocumented students without feeling like they were treading on sensitive territory. Alejandro's suggestion that some educators feel apprehensive when interacting with undocumented students echoed all of our participants' hesitation and conscientiousness when it came to revealing their status.

Participants expressed their hope and that of their families upon entering newcomer programs such as ELL, ESL, and bilingual programs. They expected that such programs would help to acclimate them to US culture and English language, and they did; however, our participants consistently agreed that they remained in these programs well beyond the time necessary to mainstream into "regular" classrooms. While some pointed to the classes within these programs as providing relatively effective, safe spaces for them and a generally effective start to their schooling experiences, they also understood these spaces as less than rigorous. Moises explained how he felt about his academic goals, and he predicted how other students envisioned their future as ESL students:

> They [teachers] don't have high ambitions for you so then you are going to be like okay this is good enough for me. I'll just get my whatever GED and then that's good enough for me. The kids—they are not going to progress. They stay in ESL forever and then they just want out. I feel if they leave ESL classes they might see a different side of the education system or something like that.

Their ESL classrooms were theoretically created to support newcomer students learning English; unfortunately, they did not promote students' retention or development of their first language or use it as a tool for learning English. Participants reported that their first language wasn't considered an asset; instead, it was usually viewed as a deficit and even a learning disability. Indeed, our participants described an "'ELL ghetto'— a sequence of courses for English-language learners that keeps them together for multiple years in classes that do not enable them to complete prerequisites for higher tracks or college" (Darling-Hammond 2010, p. 61). For example, Maria "took first grade twice and was held back the first year since I didn't know English." Her Spanish fluency was assessed as a reason for not promoting her to the next grade although she was perfectly capable of doing grade-level work.

The ways our participants made sense of educators damaging their educational experiences were shaped by the individual interactions they experienced in US classrooms. Our participants suggested that educators negatively impacted them when they made assumptions about them, ignored them, failed to leverage their linguistic and cultural knowledge, and had low expectations of them.

Maintaining Hope

Our participants indicated that hope and hopelessness ebbed and flowed through their life experiences and often simultaneously. At some points, participants felt that all hope was lost, as Carlos described:

> I knew that my outcome didn't really matter and that how much effort I put into school didn't matter because even if I got really good grades, it was more of, "Well, that's nice. But you still can't go to your dream school because there's no way that you're gonna be able to afford it even if you get a scholarship." I lacked a lot of motivation knowing I didn't have papers.

While there were many challenges that undocumented students encountered in their education, our participants remained persistently hopeful. Take Chavo, who, amidst an early tragedy, was still able to overcome academic pitfalls.

> I never excelled in my high school or in junior high. My overall GPA in high school was like a 2.7. That has a lot to do with when my mom passed away.

I was only in 8th grade. She was very much patient and always teach me. When she passed away, I kind of lost interest in school. So I was just "Eh." I mean, about our situation. So I was like, you know, [inaudible] by studying. It's like I'm not really gonna be able to go to where I wanna go because of my situation. I wasn't really trying too hard because I thought it's too late to be an honor student. I already missed a lot of information in my 9th to 10th grade years.

Katerina expressed her overall disappointment with the walls she continued to hit, including being mistreated at work due to her undocumented status, lack of options as she applied to college, and a dearth of financial assistance, as she attempted to further her education and then obtain professional work:

I felt that I couldn't fulfill my dreams anymore. I felt sad. I kind of felt disappointed. I don't know with whom or with what but I was disappointed. I still had hope though. I always had hope and faith.

Participants attributed their hopefulness primarily to one or both of their parents' relentless support of their decision-making and pursuits of furthering their education. Oftentimes, participants shared that amidst the often-stressful situations that their undocumented statuses imposed upon them, school could serve as an opportune haven. Flor shared, "I love school. I think since I was a child, for me going to school was something of a sanctuary because it was the one place where I felt consistency." Similarly, participants expressed that their parents viewed schools as safe places. Aura recalled:

I learned that I was undocumented from a very young age. I remember knowing as far back as second grade. My mom was telling me about my situation, and she made it clear for me and for all of my siblings, "stay out of trouble and just sit in school" so nothing could affect us.

For some of our participants, schools offered a sanctuary to dream and a mythological promise of a path to success and citizenship in the United States. Participants often saw schooling as their only avenue to prove their worthiness. As Luz explained, "I just really felt pressure to care about school because I knew that I needed to convince people to fund me in order go to school." This American Dream narrative came alive, deadened, and often sobered the participants' dreams. As Daniela articulated:

But I started realizing that, you know, you can't have everything. Things became simple like that. If you can't apply for financial aid when you're going to college, you can't, you can't go, you can't apply to a lot of things even some scholarships because they would ask for my social. Things like that, I think that school was my life back then so it really didn't sink in. I really didn't think about work. I didn't think of nothing in terms of time.

We found that participants lived fervently in the moment, often avoiding thoughts of the future while simultaneously accomplishing feats that would allow them to forge a path toward it. The temporal daily acts of hope such as going to school with their heads held high amidst adversity and seeking resources in times of fear and confusion kept them focused on the possibilities of today.

Discussion

We have to take a look at the ethics of our work and understand that it isn't optional to learn about undocumented students' experiences and the policies that impact them. Making assumptions that are often ill informed is irresponsible. Finding the balance between giving accurate information and being knowledgeable about outside resources is key. Coming out as undocumented is a thoughtful choice and a hard one—when a student comes out to an educator, it is a moment to be cherished and protected. Our participants' experiences are certainly not the only critical interventions and practices that undocumented students identified as pivotal to the nurturing and demise of their hope, advancement of their educational goals, and desire to pay it forward. However, they represent a sentiment attached to their undocumented reality—that when it comes down to it, educators matter, for better or for worse.

Participants described seemingly accidental encounters with a variety of educators that opened doors for them that would have otherwise remained invisible or closed—when a professor gave them the tap, encouraging them to apply to graduate school, or the community-college counselor handed them an application to a four-year institution, or a coach accompanied them on a college visit. Laura framed it as "being in the right place at the right time." The unfortunate aspect of these types of phenomenal encounters was that they tended to be random rather than the norm. The question becomes, how do we, as educators, institutionalize efforts so that all students are receiving the kind of push they need in order to have the choice of pursuing options? Certainly, there are curricular and school reforms that aim to systematically enforce equitable schooling practices. As the immigrant population continues to grow and more undocumented students come out of the shadows, it seems that waiting for policy to change, while crucially important, is not an option in the immediate now.

We can, however, turn to the daily interactions, however brief, between educators and students to foment this change. Participants were clear that caring, encouragement, hopefulness, and inspiration and the lack thereof were factors that could not be underestimated in impacting their schooling processes. The ease with which participants recalled educators that advocated for them and did damage speaks to the impact that these educators had on their lives. Laura stated that she didn't realize that she had "mentors back then but I know now that they were," suggesting that, at the time, there were educators who guided her although she was unaware of their impact until years later. As educators, we know that our work is rarely instantly gratifying, but when we hear Laura and other participants stress the importance of their past experiences with educators, we understand the nature of our work. More importantly, participants described the most impactful educators as diverse in discipline, background, race, socioeconomic class, political orientation, personality, and temperament. In other words, there was not necessarily a teacher profile that fit an effective educator, except for one characteristic: authentic care. This care took different forms and was often found in combination with other traits, including holding high academic expectations, going out of their way to help, taking part in community activism, and performing all-around positive harassment.

Participants stressed that they would rather be listened to by educators even if the educators didn't have all or any of the answers about undocumented status. The message resounded loud and clear: just being there and being present was the ultimate sign of caring. Our research echoed similar findings to that of Suárez-Orozco et al. (2010) except with a caveat. While their "data showed that students were unlikely to turn to teachers, counselors, or other adults at school for advice about getting into college" (p. 142), our participants expressed reticence to do the same unless that person showed authentic care.

CONCLUSION

Undocumented students and their families continue to live out the narrative of education as savior. Indeed, it seems only logical that an education would afford a young person everything they need to give back to the society that invested in them. Time and again, our participants held on to every last drop of hope, digging deeply into a seemingly bottomless well of aspiration, expecting that this logic might take hold—that their contributions would be met with affirmation and opportunity. But we don't live in a society of logic; instead, we live in a system where exclusivity and access are status symbols. Leaving some out deems others deserving and entitled. Coutin (2011a, b) stresses the need to attend to "the irrationalities that infuse immigration and immigration law, ranging from societal desires for an excluded other, to the deportation of community members, to the myths that motivate immigration" (p. 302).

And while undocumented students hold no guarantee that furthering their education will lead to success or citizenship, educators inevitably impact their lives whether or not furthering their education will. The fact is that within everyday interactions lies the potential for impact, be it a word of encouragement, an attentive ear, or an insistent ethic of authentic care. More importantly, we need to build an infrastructure that prepares educators for a diverse student body. As Enrique put it, "I think that it's easy to listen to the story of somebody struggling or going through hardship. We've heard so many stories that it's easy to just kind of say 'that's terrible' but then you go on with your day." As educators, we must resist this indifference and put the time in to systemically establish, nurture, and grow these personal relationships with students that build trust and open the doors to critical interventions and practices. Certainly, this can be easier said than done, given the multitude of institutional challenges that often place educators in untenable positions. Yet no matter what the environment, the potentiality in everyday interactions holds power. As Pepe said, when it comes to undocumented students, follow one simple rule: "Be there for them." We would extend Pepe's suggestion to include Valenzuela's notions of caring by saying, "Be *authentically* there for them." We could say that undocumented Latinx students are just like any other students in that they benefit from those invaluable caring student-educator relationships, but they aren't the same. Unlike other students, the stakes are much, much higher.

Acknowledgments Our deep appreciation to Ann Marie Ryan, Caleb Steindam, and Michael Dantley for their support and feedback in writing this manuscript.

REFERENCES

Abrego, L. (2006). "I can't go to college because i don't have papers": Incorporation patterns of Latino undocumented youth. *Latino Studies, 4*(3), 212–231.

Abrego, L. (2008). Legitimacy, social identity, and the mobilization of law: The effects of Assembly Bill 540 on undocumented students in California. *Law & Social Inquiry, 33*(3), 709–734.

Abrego, L. (2011). Legal consciousness of undocumented Latinos: Fear and stigma as barriers to claims making for first and 1.5 generation immigrants. *Law & Society Review, 45*(2), 337–369.

Abrego, L., & Gonzales, R. (2010). Blocked paths, uncertain futures: The post-secondary education and labor market prospects of undocumented Latino youth. *Journal of Education of Students Placed at Risk, 15*(1), 144–157.

Antrop-González, R., & De Jesús, A. (2006). Toward a theory of critical care in urban small school reform: Examining structures and pedagogies of caring in two Latino community-based schools. *International Journal of Qualitative Studies in Education, 19*(4), 409–433.

Arriaga, B. (2012). "67 Sueños": Inspiring a movement for undocumented voices to be heard. *Journal of the Association of Mexican American Educators, 6*(1), 71–76.

Bagley, C., & Castro-Salazar, R. (2012). Critical arts-based research in education: Performing undocumented historias. *British Educational Research Journal, 38*(2), 239–260.

Bozick, R., & Miller, T. (2014). In-state college tuition policies for undocumented immigrants: Implications for high school enrollment among non-citizen Mexican youth. *Population Research and Policy Review, 33*(1), 13–30. https://doi.org/10.1007/s11113-013-9307-4.

Burkhardt, J. C., Ortega, N., Vidal-Rodriguez, A., Frye, J. R., Nellum, C. J., Reyes, K. A., Hussain, O., Badke, L. K., & Hernandez, J. (2012). *Reconciling federal, state, and institutional policies determining educational access for undocumented students: Implications for professional practice.* Ann Arbor: National Forum on Higher Education for the Public Good.

Castro-Salazar, R., & Bagley, C. (2010). "Ni de Aquí ni from there." Navigating between contexts: Counter-narratives of undocumented Mexican students in the United States. *Race Ethnicity and Education, 13*(1), 23–40.

Chang, A. (2011). Undocumented to hyperdocumented: A Jornada of protection, papers and PhD status. *Harvard Educational Review, 81*(3), 508–520.

Chang, A. (2015). Privileged and undocumented: Toward a borderland love ethic. *Association of Mexican American Educators, 9*(2), 6–17.

Chang, A. (2016). Undocumented intelligence: Laying low by achieving high as a good noncitizen citizen. *Race, Ethnicity and Education.* https://doi.org/10.1 080/13613324.2016.1168539.

Chang, A., Torrez, M., Ferguson, K., & Sagar, A. (2017). Figured worlds and American dreams: An exploration of agency and identity among Latinx undocumented students. *Urban Review.* https://doi.org/10.1007/s11256-017-0397-x.

Chávez, M. L., Soriano, M., & Olivérez, P. (2007). Undocumented students' access to college: The American dream denied. *Latino Studies, 5*, 254–263. https://doi.org/10.1057/pal- grave.lst.8600255.

Chen, E. C., Budianto, L., & Wong, K. (2010). Professional school counselors as social justice advocates for undocumented immigrant students in group work. *Journal for Specialists in Group Work, 35*(3), 255–261.

Contreras, F. (2009). Sin Papeles y Rompiendo Barreras: Latino students and the challenges of persisting in college. *Harvard Educational Review, 79*(4), 610–632.

Coutin, S. B. (2003). Borderlands, illegality and the spaces of non-existence. In R. Perry & B. Maurer (Eds.), *Globalization and governmentalities* (pp. 171–202). Minneapolis: University of Minnesota Press.

Coutin, S. B. (2005). Contesting criminality: Illegal immigration and the spatialization of legality. *Theoretical Criminology, 9*(1), 5–33.

Coutin, S. B. (2010). Exiled by law: Deportation and the inviability of life. In N. De Genova & N. Peutz (Eds.), *The deportation regime: Sovereignty, space, and the freedom of movement.* Durham: Duke University Press.

Coutin, S. B. (2011a). The rights of non-citizens in the United States. *Annual Review of Law & Social Science, 7*, 289–308.

Coutin, S. B. (2011b). Legal exclusion and dislocated subjectivities: The deportation of Salvadoran youth from the United States. In V. J. Squire (Ed.), *The contested politics of mobility: Borderzones and irregularity* (pp. 169–181). London: Routledge.

Coutin, S. B. (2013). In the breach: Citizenship and its approximations. *Indiana Journal of Global Legal Studies, 20*(1), 109–140.

Covarrubias, A., & Lara, A. (2014). The undocumented (im)migrant educational pipeline: The influence of citizenship status on educational attainment for people of Mexican origin. *Urban Education, 49*(1), 75–110.

Darling-Hammond, L. (2010). *The flat world and education: How America's commitment to equity will determine our future.* New York: Teacher's College Press.

De Genova, N. P. (2002). Migrant 'illegality' and deportability in everyday life. *Annual Review of Anthropology, 31*, 419–437.

De Genova, N. (2005). *Working the boundaries: Race, space, and "illegality" in Mexican Chicago.* Durham: Duke University Press.

De Genova, N. (2006). *Racial transformations: Latinos and Asians remaking the United States.* Durham: Duke University Press.

De Genova, N., & Peutz, N. (2010). *The deportation regime: Sovereignty, space, and the freedom of movement.* Durham: Duke University Press.

De Genova, N., & Ramos-Zayas, A. Y. (2003). *Latino crossings: Mexicans, Puerto Ricans, and the politics of race and citizenship.* New York: Routledge.

De Jesús, A., & Antrop-González, R. (2006). Instrumental relationships and high expectations: Exploring critical care in two Latino community-based schools. *Intercultural Education, 17*(3), 281–299.

Diaz-Strong, D., Gomez, C., Luna-Duarte, M. E., & Meiners, E. R. (2011). Purged: Undocumented students, financial aid policies, and access to higher education. *Journal of Hispanic Higher Education, 10*(2), 107–119.

Dougherty, K. J., Nienhusser, H. K., & Vega, B. (2010). Undocumented immigrants and state higher education policy: The politics of in-state tuition eligibility in Texas and Arizona. *Review of Higher Education, 34*(1), 123–173.

Dozier, S. B. (2001). Undocumented and documented international students: A comparative study of their academic performance. *Community College Review, 29*(2), 43–53. https://doi.org/10.1177/009155210102900204.

Duncan-Andrade, J. M. R. (2009). Note to educators: Hope required when growing roses in concrete. *Harvard Educational Review, 79*(2), 181–194.

Ellis, L. M., & Chen, E. C. (2013). Negotiating identity development among undocumented immigrant college students: A grounded theory study. *Journal of Counseling Psychology, 60*(2), 251–264.

Enriquez, L. E. (2011). 'Because we feel the pressure and we also feel the support': Examining the educational success of undocumented immigrant Latina/o students. *Harvard Educational Review, 81*(3), 476–500.

Enriquez, L. E. (2014). "Undocumented and citizen students unite": Building a cross-status coalition through shared ideology. *Social Problems, 61*(2), 155–174. https://doi.org/10.1525/sp.2014.12032.

Flores, S. (2010). State dream acts: The effect of in-state resident tuition policies and undocumented Latino students. *Review of Higher Education, 38*(1), 239–283.

Flores, S. M., & Horn, C. L. (2009). College persistence among undocumented students at a selective public university: A quantitative case study analysis. *Journal of College Student Retention: Research, Theory and Practice, 11*(1), 57–76.

Fontana, A., & Frey, J. H. (2000). The interview—From structured questions to negotiated text. In N. Denzin & Y. Lincoln (Eds.), *Handbook of qualitative research* (pp. 645–672). Thousand Oaks: Sage.

Galindo, R. (2011). Embodying the gap between national inclusion and exclusion: The congressional testimony of three undocumented students. *Harvard Latino Law Review, 14*, 377–395.

Galindo, R. (2012). Undocumented & unafraid: The DREAM Act 5 and the public disclosure of undocumented status as a political act. *Urban Review: Issues and Ideas in Public Education, 44*(5), 589–611.

Garcia, L. D., & Tierney, W. G. (2011). Undocumented immigrants in higher education: A preliminary analysis. *Teachers College Record, 113*(12), 2739–2776.

Glenn, E. (2011). Constructing citizenship: Exclusion, subordination, and resistance. *American Sociological Review, 76*(1), 1–24.

Gonzales, R. (2009). Special report: Young lives on hold: The college dreams of undocumented students. *The College Board*, 1–27.

Gonzales, R. G. (2010). On the wrong side of the tracks: Understanding the effects of school structure and social capital in the educational pursuits of undocumented immigrant students. *Peabody Journal of Education, 85*(4), 46.

Hernandez, I., Mendoza, F., Lio, M., Latthi, J., & Eusebio, C. (2011). Things I'll never say: Stories of growing up undocumented in the United States. *Harvard Educational Review, 81*(3), 500–508.

Huber, L. P. (2010). Using Latina/o critical race theory (LatCrit) and racist nativism to explore intersectionality in the educational experiences of undocumented Chicana college students. *Educational Foundations, 24*(1–2), 77–96.

Huber, L. P., & Malagon, M. C. (2007). Silenced struggles: The experiences of Latina and Latino undocumented college students in California. *The Nevada Journal, 7*, 841–861.

Huber, L. P., Malagon, M. C., & Solorzano, D. G. (2009). *Struggling for opportunity: Undocumented AB 540 students in the Latina/o education pipeline* (CSRC research report no. 13). UCLA Chicano Studies Research Center.

Jacobo, R., & Ochoa, A. M. (2011). Examining the experiences of undocumented college students: Walking the known and unknown lived spaces. *Journal of the Association of Mexican American Educators, 5*(1), 22–30.

King, K. A., & Punti, G. (2012). On the margins: Undocumented students' narrated experiences of (il)legality. *Linguistics and Education: An International Research Journal, 23*(3), 235–249.

Lincoln, Y., & Guba, E. G. (1985). *Naturalistic inquiry*. Beverly Hills: Sage.

Lopez, J. (2010). *Undocumented students and the policies of wasted potential*. El Paso: LFB Scholarly Publishing.

Madison, D. S. (2005). *Critical ethnography: Method, ethics and performance*. Thousand Oaks: Sage.

Menjívar, C., & Abrego, L. (2009). Parents and children across borders: Legal instability and intergenerational relations in Guatemalan and Salvadoran families. In N. Foner (Ed.), *Across generations: Immigrant families in America* (pp. 160–189). New York: New York University Press.

Muñoz, S. (2015). *Identity, social activism, and the pursuit of higher education: The journey stories of undocumented and unafraid community activists*. New York: Peter Lang.

Nguyen, D. K., & Serna, G. R. (2014). Access or barrier? Tuition and fee legislation for undocumented students across the States. *Clearing House, 87*(3), 124–129. https://doi.org/10.1080/00098655.2014.891895.

Nienhusser, H. K. (2014). Role of community colleges in the implementation of postsecondary education enrollment policies for undocumented students. *Community College Review, 42*(1), 3–22. https://doi.org/10.1177/0091552113509837.

Olivas, M. A. (2012). *No undocumented child left behind: Plyler v. Doe and the education of undocumented schoolchildren*. New York: New York University Press.

Orner, P. (2008). *Underground America: Narratives of undocumented lives*. San Francisco: McSweeney's.

Ortiz, A. M., & Hinojosa, A. (2010). Tenuous options: The career development process for undocumented students. *New Directions for Student Services, 131*, 53–65.

Patel, L. (2013). *Youth held at the border: Immigration, education, and the politics of inclusion*. New York: Teachers College Press.

Patton, M. Q. (1990). *Qualitative evaluation and research methods*. Newbury Park: Sage.

Pérez, W. (2009). *We are Americans*. Sterling: Stylus.

Pérez, P. A. (2010a). College choice process of Latino undocumented students: Implications for recruitment and retention. *Journal of College Admission, 206*, 21–25.

Pérez, W. (2010b). Higher education access for undocumented students: Recommendations for counseling professionals. *Journal of College Admission, 206*, 32–35.

Pérez, W. (2012). *Americans by heart: Undocumented Latino students and the promise of higher education*. New York: Teachers College Press.

Pérez, P. A., & Rodriguez, J. L. (2011). Access and opportunity for Latina/o undocumented college students: Familial and institutional support factors. *Journal of the Association of Mexican American Educators, 5*(1), 14–21.

Pérez, W., Espinoza, R., Ramos, K., Coronado, H. M., & Cortes, R. (2009). Academic resilience among undocumented Latino students. *Hispanic Journal of Behavioral Sciences, 31*(2), 149–181.

Rincon, A. (2010). Si se puede!: Undocumented immigrants' struggle for education and their right to stay. *Journal of College Admission, 206*, 13–18.

Rodriguez, G. M., & Cruz, L. (2009). The transition to college of English learner and undocumented immigrant students: Resource and policy implications. *Teachers College Record, 111*(10), 2385–2418.

Román, E. (2013). *Those damned immigrants: America's hysteria over undocumented immigration*. New York: New York University Press.

Ryscavage, R., & Canaris, M. M. (2013). Undocumented students ask Jesuit higher ed: 'Just us' or justice? *New England Journal of Higher Education*. Retrieved from: http://www.nebhe.org/thejournal/undocumented-students-ask-jesuit-higher-education-just-us-or-justice/

Storlie, C. A., & Jach, E. A. (2012). Social justice collaboration in schools: A model for working with undocumented Latino students. *Journal for Social Action in Counseling & Psychology, 4*(2), 99–116.

Suárez-Orozco, C., Suárez-Orozco, M. M., & Todorova, I. (2010). *Learning a new land: Immigrant students in American society*. Cambridge, MA: Belknap Press of Harvard University Press.

Torres, R., & Wicks-Asbun, M. (2014). Undocumented students' narratives of liminal citizenship: High aspirations, exclusion, and 'in-between' identities. *Professional Geographer, 66*(2), 195–204. https://doi.org/10.1080/0033012 4.2012.735936.

Valenzuela, A. (1999). *Subtractive schooling: U.S.-Mexican youth and the politics of caring*. Albany: State University of New York Press.

Vargas, E. D. (2011). In-state tuition policies for undocumented youth. *Harvard Journal of Hispanic Policy, 23*, 43–58.

Viramontez Anguiano, R. P., & Lopez, A. (2012). 'El miedo y el hambre': Understanding the familial, social, and educational realities of undocumented Latino families in North Central Indiana. *Journal of Family Social Work, 15*(4), 321–336.

CHAPTER 6

Working with Undocumented Students: What They Say We Need to Know

Many educators rightfully lack confidence when working with undocumented students. Their apprehension comes from a variety of sources. Some fear that "aiding and abetting" an undocumented person is a crime. Others lack knowledge around the technicalities of immigration: the process of obtaining citizenship, immigration law, resources for undocumented students, and current relevant legislation. Overall, most folks fear that they will not know how to respond in a helpful way, at best, and give harmful advice, at worst. Their intentions are predominantly good but good intentions do not always translate to good practice. So, they either give these students poor advice, avoid giving advice altogether, or refer them to someone else. Rather than guessing what to say, it is important that we hear directly from undocumented students about what is truly helpful for them. In this chapter, I will draw from my most recent research data to provide a bit of advice to those who work with undocumented students. This is not legal advice or a "how to become a citizen" guide (as if there were such a thing). Rather, this is advice from undocumented students telling us what we need to know in order to be effective in helping them navigate the daily challenges they encounter because of their immigration status.

Over the past two years, I have been conducting in-depth youth participatory action research (YPAR) with four undocumented students that focuses on their identity, education, and agency. For some context, YPAR is research about, by, and for its youth participants. YPAR opens the role

© The Author(s) 2018   109
A. Chang, *The Struggles of Identity, Education,*
and Agency in the Lives of Undocumented Students,
https://doi.org/10.1007/978-3-319-64614-5_6

of researcher to students "as subjects and partners" in conducting research (Duncan-Andrade and Morrell 2008, p. 108). Rather than research being done on young people, YPAR students are positioned as the experts of their community cultural wealth, their experiences, and their schooling processes. Unlike traditional research approaches, YPAR students participate in every aspect of the research process. Through this experience, YPAR students learn new research skills, develop academic language, and begin to experiment with and initiate theory. They study issues that are relevant and meaningful to them and then apply those research findings to collectively take action to work toward social justice (Scott et al. 2014; McIntyre 2000). YPAR students are agents and producers of knowledge. YPAR is a powerful foundation for yielding knowledge that is authentically caring because it demonstrates the deepest regard for students' intellect and lived experiences. Here, I present some of what I have learned through this research.

With a backdrop of YPAR students' basic portraits and anecdotes, I present three pieces of general advice through the words of undocumented students:

1. You don't need to know a lot to help me.
2. Don't tell me everything is going to be fine.
3. Walk the path alongside me.

Let me emphasize here that there are a variety of ways to support undocumented students and that we must do so at every front. Here, I discuss interpersonal ways of helping rather than policy-related or systemic approaches to change. This is not because I undervalue such approaches. On the contrary, we need people from all walks of life, all backgrounds, and all areas of expertise to participate in this struggle. The reasons why I focus on the everyday interactions among educators and undocumented students are threefold. First, this is what I know best. My expertise is not on public policy but rather on the everyday agentic actions that feed a life of meaning and contribute to socially just efforts. Second, for those of us who often feel overwhelmed by the grandiosity of politics and feel paralyzed by an inability to affect change in "large" ways, this advice can be immediately implemented and requires no outside knowledge beyond self-reflection and a bit of vulnerability. Finally, these pieces of advice are meant to be returned to, time and time again when you feel helpless or ignorant in the face of an undocumented student's struggle, frustration, and pain.

You Don't Need to Know a Lot to Help Me

My first memory of being undocumented is clearly seared in my body. I must have been somewhere between first and fourth grade. My mama was registering me for the first day of school. We must have arrived at an off-hour because we were the only ones in the elementary school office with Ms. B, the school secretary. She was familiar to me because we had often sat next to her at mass in the St Callistus Churchpew on Sunday mornings. When I was filling out the registration paperwork, I asked mama what 'SSN' meant. She and Ms B exchanged glances. Ms B said, 'Write your tax id number,' which I knew by heart, having used it many times before on different types of forms. My mama gave silent thanks in the meek and heartfelt way that only she knew how to express. Something powerful happened in that subtle exchange. I knew my mama and Ms. B had made an arrangement of sorts, the way a child looks up at two adults and knows that a secret was shared and an understanding was established. Nothing I learned within school walls was as powerful and consequential as the tacit lessons that were so effectively inculcated in me as an undocumented immigrant from Guatemala. Ms. B was not any sort of expert on immigration. All she knew was that a five-year-old kid of a church friend of hers needed to go to school and she could make that happen. She didn't need to know a lot to help me. Undocumented students seem to indicate that they are aware of the different human resources they can access. When they go to educators, they are not seeking legal advice or even practical suggestions; they seek to be heard attentively. They go to you because they trust you as a fellow human being who can lend an ear, a compassionate eye, and a kind word.

One of the best phrases you can utter to any student is "I don't know." The act of expressing ignorance, incertitude, and vulnerability sends a powerful message to students. It demonstrates that educators are not all-knowing, that it is acceptable and even encouraged to show doubt, and models what students should say when they feel unsure. Specifically, for undocumented students, doling out advice that is misinformed can have catastrophic consequences. For example, if an undocumented student asks you a question about a legal form or a decision they need to make regarding their immigration status, and you are not an immigration lawyer, your most authentically caring response should be something along the lines of, "I can imagine how stressful this must be for you. I don't know the answer but I will find at least one resource that may be able to help you with that. And I will be right here to listen every step of the way."

Or listen to Luis, one of my student co-researchers, who describes an interaction he had with a college counselor. Luis is an undocumented community college student who faced a torrent of struggles over the past year. He is one of those people that always has a smile on his face and is ready to provide a hug. He is five feet tall, stocky, with a small frame. His hair is always meticulously gelled in the right direction and his clothes always well pressed and easily coordinated. Luis is always open to listening. His peers open up to him with ease but he hardly takes up any space for his own highs and lows. As he struggled to write his personal statement to transfer to a four-year university from community college, he shared his experience with Ms. White.

I think for me, personally, I hadn't realized how hard this would be. I tried to start my paper, but it just brought up so many memories and so many things. I just ended up closing my laptop. I'm like, not today. So, I came and I met with Ms. White. And I had like a two-hour conversation with this amazing person. She basically helped me brainstorm how to use my weaknesses as strengths. Something that I saw that was so negative and dark, she was just like, this is probably good to write about, as much as it hurts, you know. I am undocumented. My family has struggled. I lost my brother in April. During this time, I wasn't doing so well, you know, losing somebody so close, somebody that's always been there for you, somebody you look up to. You know, it's not something I want somebody else to experience. Also, I was in a really bad relationship that also around this time came to an end. And you know, I had all these feelings, all these emotions that I just didn't know how to get them out. I kept it all inside.

People see me smiling; people see me happy all the time. I'm always so welcoming and, you know, full of joy, I guess. But sometimes, there's sides of people that you just never show. Everything went downhill after my brother passed away, to be honest. Because you're just full of questions. Why do things happen, you know? It just really affects you. In a way, you kind of get the idea of why you want to do the things you do. After so much that has happened to me, why do I still want to help people? Why do I want to go into the medical field? Why do I care for other people? After people that I don't even know have hurt me so bad, you know? It's like things I wouldn't regularly talk about. I try to avoid subjects like that because they just bring back really bad memories. So, I guess I kind of have to get out of my comfort zone and talk about these things. And just, as much as there is to write about and to remember and to try to put it on paper, I just don't know how. Honestly, I just don't know where to begin. Something so simple as this that you just, it turns into something so big. I kind of have a sense, but I don't know how to get it out. I lost my brother, this relationship gone bad. I also got robbed like really badly. They stole the car, they stole my wallet, they stole my phone. But all of this going on and still trying to do well in school. But in the end, I still finished off with a 3.0. And where did I get the strength to work on that, I don't know. But I think that's one of my biggest strengths. After everything that was going on, I still managed to get somewhat good grades in school. I just didn't know how to put that on paper. Ms. White helped me do that.

In this case, Luis presented Ms. White with a variety of intersecting issues, one of which was being undocumented. Ms. White didn't need to know anything about what it means to be undocumented or a lot about any particular issue to help him. Her knowledge of the stages of grief, post-traumatic stress, relationship management, coping mechanisms, or immigration status was less necessary than the simple act of spending two hours out of her day listening to and being with Luis—allowing him a space to use his own skills and tools to process his struggles. In that process, Ms. White honored and encouraged Luis' abilities to think critically and nurture his intuitive wherewithal. She didn't need to know a lot to help him and her help proved invaluable.

Don't Tell Me Everything Is Going to Be Fine

Remember my tenth-grade experience with Girls' State when I was denied the opportunity to exercise "responsible citizenship and love for God and country" (see Chap. 2) when my chance to participate in Girls' State was revoked? If a teacher would have known about my status and just told me to go ahead and apply because everything was going to be alright, that would have been inauthentic caring. The second piece of advice is, don't tell me everything is going to be fine. Because it may not be fine.

Take Jorge, one of my co-researchers, an undocumented student who, by every account, is a high achiever, community leader, and kind human being. Jorge is difficult to describe because every adjective seems to fall short of his uniqueness. Standing at about five feet, he has a runner's build—compact, light, and airy. The first thing you notice about him, after his glowing smile, is the patchy wisps of hair on his almost balding head. There is an immediate humility to him. His eyes are honest. He was my first YPAR student co-researcher and the one who connected me to our other student co-researchers. Wickedly savvy and the academic golden boy of his community college, Jorge often sought the advice of his professors and school administration.

One interaction he highlighted involved one of his favorite professors, Mr. Bill. Mr. Bill was a clean-cut, white, middle-aged, preppy professor of English. He always had something funny to say and was very eager to listen to students' stories and learn from their experiences. Although Mr. Bill grew up in an upper-class suburb, he worked very hard to relate to his students of color by engaging in culturally relevant practices he had learned from a series of professional development experiences. A few days after Donald Trump was elected, Jorge was having one of many casual conversations with Mr. Bill. Jorge was overwhelmed with shock, anger, and fear anticipating the draconian immigration policies which were inevitably over the horizon. He explained his worry, given that he was undocumented. Although he was a DACA recipient, he now feared the worst. Would it be possible that the information he disclosed to apply for DACA would then be used to deport him? Mr. Bill listened with concern and perhaps, unable to find the best thing to say, responded to Jorge by saying "Don't worry. Everything will be okay." Jorge was taken aback by this seemingly nonchalant response. Mr. Bill spoke with a certainty that was unfounded. Of course, Jorge was going to worry and there was no guarantee that everything would be okay. While Jorge understood that Mr. Bill was trying to say the right thing, he lost some trust in him. Jorge felt that the suggestion that everything would be okay was less than sincere. How could Mr. Bill say that, knowing that Jorge could be deported? He was disappointed in Mr. Bill's quick consolation; it was no consolation at all. On the contrary, it made Jorge feel leery of approaching Mr. Bill in the future.

One of the things that undocumented students tell me is that they feel dismissed and discouraged when their teachers and counselors reassure them that everything is going to be fine. How do they know? Students have told me that they think this may make the teachers and counselors feel better, but what it seems to communicate to them as students is that the person is either ignorant of the realities of their undocumented circumstances, in a rush to say something, anything so they say something seemingly soothing but lacking in thoughtfulness, or feeling pity toward them and therefore giving them false consolation. It is okay, even encouraging, to communicate that everything may not be alright so long as you are willing to take on the responsibility of seeing the student through their struggle. This tells students that you are aware of the possibilities, that you care enough to be realistic, and that you will support them.

WALK THE PATH ALONGSIDE ME

Maria and Ahmed, two of my co-researchers, recently shared two stories that illustrate the importance of walking alongside undocumented students. The key word here is alongside. Undocumented students don't need educators to walk in front of them in a paternalistic fashion, treating them as obedient children. Undocumented students don't need educators to walk behind them, looking over their shoulders or being there to catch their falls. Undocumented students need educators to walk alongside them as equal partners in a struggle that lacks simple answers and presents no immediate end in sight. It is easy to say you will walk alongside an undocumented student but will you be there when they get served by ICE (Immigration and Customs Enforcement), when they are stopped at the border, when they are detained at an immigrant prison, when their lack of financial aid prevents them from attending college, when one of their parents is deported, when they are pulled over without a license, when they are unable to travel abroad, when they need a plate of food or a place to stay? Here, I briefly introduce Maria and Ahmed as they offer us lessons to consider in our work with undocumented students.

MARIA AND THE FAKE ID

When I saw Maria for the first time, she reminded me of an avatar. Her big, round, enveloping eyes are dark brown, almost black. Her shiny hair, done up in the most precise tresses, hangs easily below her waist. She is probably one hundred pounds soaking wet. There is a shyness to her teethy smile and an eagerness for knowledge that is palpable. Everyone admires her beauty, her dancing skills, and her outright ferocious intellect. She has made the Dean's list each year, has a full ride to the four-year university she has aspired to attend, and she is undocumented.

Maria remembers every detail of her immigration. She was 15 when she made the trek. Living in Guatemala, she and her family were in imminent danger. Death threats against she and her sisters began, so the family strategically began to move from rural location to rural location, running from the inevitable death threats that would follow them. If you are unfamiliar with the politics of Latin America or Guatemala, this may seem dramatic and unusual. But, for someone like me, who was born in Guatemala and whose family members predominantly still live there, kidnappings, killings, ransoms, and death threats are the stuff of everyday life.

I have had cousins and uncles who have been kidnapped for ransom. My own family received death threats. While Maria and I grew up at different ends of the socioeconomic spectrum, the violence of Guatemala still impacted us both.

As Maria and her siblings moved from place to place, there was a moment when her grandmother and her mother's family could no longer take care of them—the threat of danger was too overwhelming and they wanted nothing to do with it. Maria's mother and father were already in the United States, setting up home so that their children could then join them. They had also immigrated to the United States due to violent threats. Upon hearing of the intense danger that was upon her daughters, Maria's mother moved back to Guatemala, but that only exacerbated an already tense situation. When Maria's mother's threatener learned of her whereabouts, he threatened to kill her and her daughters. She escaped Guatemala, leaving her daughters there with a plan to eventually meet up in El Norte.

Crossing to El Norte, however, meant money—the costs of a coyote, primarily. But Maria didn't have money so she borrowed money from family members who knew Mexico and with their assistance prepared to cross the Guatemala/Mexico border. Maria was so relieved to know that she would be leaving Guatemala. It was like she was heading to a vacation. They crossed two rivers and walked a lot. When they finally made it to Mexico, they were approached by a coyote who assured them that he would take them to the United States at a good price. Everything seemed to be going as planned and Maria was full of hope. They were able to put together half of the money through various personal loans. The coyote put them on the bus and waved good bye. But, like many immigrants who have crossed before, their hopes were stolen.

When the bus arrived in Tijuana, the coyote wasn't there but bandits awaited, ransacked the bus and stole all the passengers' money and possessions. Maria was able to keep some of her money that she had stealthily packed in the corners of her clothes she wore but that was it. No one was there. Maria and her family were disoriented and got lost. They had no one. They had nothing. I was the only one that could save some money because I had candy apples. For days, they couldn't communicate with their father in the United States. They slept in the bus terminal. Desperate, Maria's mom encountered a kind-looking man in the station and came up with a lie. She relayed that they were in Tijuana to visit a friend who was not reachable. So, he invited us to his home until we could figure out our next step. And so, the four of us stayed with him for several months.

They spent those months trying to figure out how to cross the US/Mexico border. Finally, they found someone who was willing to cross her little sisters. The coyote said that he was willing to cross them because of their young ages. Because of their small sizes and their ability to pass as children of another family, they were convenient candidates for crossing. The problem was Maria. No one wanted to cross her because she was older, 15 years old. Some people were willing to cross her at a price of $10,000. They wanted to cross together, so they stayed in Tijuana.

They slept in different houses, wherever they could find shelter or people who were kind enough to take them in. They garnered the courage to cross with a group of people. Upon reaching the border, Mexican border patrol agents stopped the whole group. They deported all the people that were with them but left Maria, her mom, and her sisters alone. The border patrol agents didn't ask for any documentation. Maria figured that they avoided being checked because they did not "look Mexican." Then, one of the border patrol agents next to her said, "I'm going to let you cross. It's fine. You are going to cross with someone." I was relieved. But at the last minute, he said, "No, you are going to cross alone." Maria tensed up. As she froze, she noticed the girl in front of her who had just crossed—she looked like her, was about the same age. At that moment, she got the courage to go, "Okay, I'll go across." Maria was nervous but when she crossed over, an amazing calm came over her.

Maria has lived in Chicago for the past five years. Her relationship with her parents has a history of being severely strained but she has managed to find a place to live, get full funding to attend community college, and will graduate with her associate's degree this August. Then, she is on her way to a four-year university where she was awarded a full scholarship. Although she is not eligible for DACA, she has done everything in her power to access resources and opportunities.

A few months ago, Maria asked if she could speak with me after our weekly group research meeting. With a concerned look on her face, she wanted my advice. Maria said, "There is a job available as a food server. My cousin arranged it and everything, but there is only one problem. They won't pay me unless I have papers." Maria paused, looked down then quickly up and asked, "So, my question is, do you think I should buy a fake id?"

Here she was, living with ten other people to save on rent, barely able to buy enough food to keep her energy up for school, disowned from her family, and doing everything in her power to just show up ... to life. So, do I think she should get a fake id? Do YOU think she should get a fake id? Do I think Maria should eat? Do YOU think Maria should eat? Do I think Maria should commit an illegal act? Do YOU think Maria should commit an illegal act? Do I think I am in a position to be giving such advice? Do YOU think you are in a position to be giving such advice? I said the first thing that came to my mouth, "I don't know what you should do but whatever you decide, I'm with you."

I don't know if that was the "right" thing to say. I never know if I am saying the "right" thing. The only thing I know for sure is the right disposition to have. Just being there, my fellow student researchers tell me, is enough, sometimes more than enough.

AHMED AND THE MAYOR

Walk the path alongside me, not in front of me or behind me. This is what I surmised from Ahmed, one of my YPAR student co-researchers, when he described a once in a lifetime opportunity to meet with the city's mayor. As I write this book, the topic of illegal immigration and the study of undocumented students have become popularized, even trendy with institutions, researchers, and media outlets taking advantage of every undocumented person to get the sexy story. Ahmed warns against this type of exploitation. Behind every media opportunity, there is a life full or hardships and hopes—something that shouldn't be taken for granted or, worse, abused. In the following excerpt, I present a composite narrative taken directly from one of Ahmed and my many discussions together.

So my principal called me and told me there was an opportunity to meet with the mayor and I told him that I would call him back later. I thought about it for about an hour, contemplating my schedule and this once in a lifetime opportunity. I figured that it wouldn't hurt to meet him. I could ask him questions and maybe tell my story. So, I show up to the mayor's house and there were a bunch of high school kids and only one college kid aside from me. So, his family was nice and all but he just asked us straightforward questions, asking us to share our stories. But, I didn't feel like he was genuine. This is how he acted. He would point to one of us and say, "You. where are you from? When did you get here? What does your father do?" So, all of us would answer his questions but there wasn't enthusiasm or anything from him. There was also no point where I could ask my questions. And he just kept asking us how our parents felt about the city being a sanctuary city. He talked about Trump and how he didn't know what he was doing as President. All of a sudden, we were following the mayor outside the stairs of his house and media was everywhere. Protesters were also out there. We were his poster kids for promoting the sanctuary city. The minute I saw that scene outside, I thought, oh my God, I'm on the wrong side of the mayor's house here! They brought us here so it looks like we are behind the mayor. I learned a lot about politics that day. It was the low of my year. I learned that you can't trust politicians at all. I learned that people just do things just for their own sake.

I thought, if I had the opportunity I would say something like, "I think this shows that we need to expand the sanctuary cities." I would have invited the mayor to listen to those requests and listen to those problems and address those issues as soon as possible. I came prepared to make this speech but I never got the chance to talk, so I would call that some purposeful scheming. So, the good part of this story is that I was able to meet the mayor's secretary. We exchanged phone numbers in case I wanted to "follow up with the mayor." She texted me the following morning at 7am. Long story short, I suggested that the mayor should host a meet and greet where the protestors could talk to the mayor. She suggested that I also join the discussion and bring my friends. She continued to text me about how they were trying to get in contact with the protestors to get this going. She sent me another email later but I didn't feel like engaging with her because I felt like I was just another student that she was trying to get to make the mayor look good. So, I decide to just express what I thought. I didn't try to modify my language to sweeten what I was saying because I had to tell her the reality of her boss. I had to tell her that, look, a lot of people don't feel listened to by the mayor. Her response was we could arrange an individual meeting with the mayor to work through this. The whole experience left me disappointed. I told my mom that I think a lot of people think try to use my niceness to their own advantage, you know? Sometimes I modify my tone to make others feel better and adjust myself according to them, but, I should not.

We must trust in the undocumented intelligence and agency of the students we work with. They do not come to us as blank slates or empty vessels to be filled with our supposed knowledge or advice. We are not their saviors. In fact, so many of these students could teach us a thing or two about survival, resilience, and navigation. We must be facilitators of that emotional, intellectual, and experiential intelligence. We need to stop pretending that we will "save" them or even "guide" them. While they live with a burden of perfectionism temporarily quelled by hyperdocumentation, our aim should be to equip students with the tools to live lives of meaning regardless of the final outcome of their citizenship status.

REFERENCES

Duncan-Andrade, J. M. R., & Morrell, E. (2008). *The art of critical pedagogy: Possibilities for moving from theory to practice in urban schools.* New York: Peter Lang.

McIntyre, A. (2000). Constructing meaning about violence, school, and community: Participatory action research with urban youth. *The Urban Review, 32*(2), 123–154.

Scott, M. A., Pyne, K. B., & Means, D. R. (2014). Approaching praxis: YPAR as critical pedagogical process in a college access program. *The High School Journal, 98*(Winter), 138–157.

CHAPTER 7

Academic Agency and the Burden of Perfectionism

In this chapter, I offer my thoughts around academic agency and the burden of perfectionism that undocumented students face. Drawing from the borderland love ethic framework, I conclude by reconnecting my own personal experiences as once undocumented to now hyperdocumented immigrant to those of the participants, drawing conclusions and posing questions for researchers to ponder. Finally, I encourage readers to enact their own agency by writing themselves into academia.

Undocumented students' pursuit of academic perfection and self-fashioning of infallible cultural citizen are survival strategies that, while in no way guarantee a path to citizenship, provide a redemptive alternative to hopelessness in the face of unthinkable odds. Undocumented students are able to figure their own worlds, find identity in their education, and leverage community cultural wealth by exploiting the one thing that remains relatively accessible—academic achievement. Hyperdocumenting may not lead to the acquisition of official papers but it can affirm their undocumented intelligence, their seemingly endless well of critical hope, and the potential of their agency.

With each victory that each undocumented student that I know has achieved, I am equally haunted by a deep realization about the prospects of their future and by my own skepticism of what their futures might hold. When four of my students shared the news that they received full rides to a prestigious and, needless to say, expensive institution, I was overwhelmed

© The Author(s) 2018
A. Chang, *The Struggles of Identity, Education, and Agency in the Lives of Undocumented Students,*
https://doi.org/10.1007/978-3-319-64614-5_7

with joy. That joy was quickly tempered by a realization that every step closer to earning their baccalaureate degree was also a step closer to limbo (Gonzales 2015). Without papers, what would they do upon graduation? Even more immediate than that, with the draconian immigration policies, would they be deported before even beginning their fall semesters? All this hype about doing well and achieving academically seemed futile in the face of all of this. What is our responsibility in taking students down this mythological path of papers? Also, how do I continue to feed into this hyper-documentation hustle as an academic? There are still so many unanswered questions.

Undocumented students' approach to their dilemma of immigration status teaches us a valuable lesson about the power of mindfulness and the reality of process. The undocumented students I worked with were not waiting on citizenship status to start their lives. Instead, they lived in the moment, believing in the inherent value of doing good by themselves, their families, and their communities. Of course, they worried over what was to come but this angst created momentum for them; it did not stunt them. So, what if they didn't gain citizenship—would they change the daily ways in which they live their lives? Staying as present as they could, they focused on the now. They wrote their papers for classes, volunteered at church, tutored at the local Y, joined dance club, ran for office, applied for scholarships, ran errands for their parents, accompanied their younger siblings to school events, ran 5K's, attended lectures, and advocated for themselves and others. Where the process led was ultimately not as important as how the process was experienced—the friends they made along the way, the family members they made proud, the sense of self-efficacy they developed, the knowledge they gained, the teachers they learned from, the contributions they made to efforts of social justice. Throughout my work with these students, I often had to stop and remind myself that my intention was not to get them to become citizens, though that would obviously be a welcome outcome. In fact, whatever my imagined goals were for such research, at the end of the day, their goals and development held the greatest value.

In my own case, as a once undocumented immigrant who still hyper-documents, I often found myself writing up the next journal article in my head, considering grant deadlines for funding of this research, stressing over when transcriptions of interviews would be completed and the like. I am reminded of the ways in which my own hyperdocumented identity remains with me. As I write this chapter, I have just completed reviewing my course evaluations for this past semester. I received the worst evaluations ever from one of my courses. In my quest to be the perfect scholar, teacher, editor, and speaker, I relearned a valuable lesson that seemed to reemerge every once in a while. Hyperdocumentation has its limits, often reached when one part of your life has to give in order to make time for everything else. Even more importantly though is the significance of overall wellness.

I realized after a full year of meeting with the undocumented students I worked with on a weekly basis, that I had not once just paused to ask them about their mental health. Each week, we were getting to work—developing research questions, writing reflections, working on college applications, researching scholarship funding, writing letters to senators and congress people, revising essays for philosophy class, discussing the political despair of the day. We were hyperdocumenting and I was leading that hyperdocumentation frenzy. In the end, would it have been better to simply look in each of their eyes, and ask, "How ARE you?" We went around sharing highs and lows each week, but as the weeks passed, I could literally see the damage of stress, hopelessness, sleepless nights, food scarcity, financial need, and overall weight in the droopiness of their eyelids, the slouching of their backs, their complaints of stomach pains, never-ending colds, and unwavering anxiety. Yet, even under those circumstances, I modeled what I had practiced at their age and before; I pushed them to the edge of overachievement. As we stayed in our meeting room past the hours where the intercampus shuttle ran, editing yet another paper of some sort via google docs, I was recreating that barracks of library books but now it was a virtual barracks of laptop screens, phone apps, and tablets. Perhaps I could avoid the reality of their suffering by perpetuating the American myth of individualism and meritocracy. I know I wasn't doing this purposefully and it was the only way I knew how to be alive and not allow the pessimism always at the tip of my fingers to ominously cast a spell on us. My fear was, if I allowed the pain to be exposed, would the pain ever stop? I didn't want that for them or perhaps I was being selfish— it wasn't so much about them as it was about me. After all, how would I contain that pain, what did I know about the deep messiness of insecurity, the tug of war of hope and despair, the possibilities of materialized nightmares? As it turns out, I knew a lot about that.

In my childhood home, I used hyperdocumentation to lay low by achieving high, but I also used it as an avoidance technique. I didn't want to face what was happening in my own family—the always impending divorce of my parents, the constant fear of my father's moods, and the deep insecurity

I felt as a child, never knowing what new tragedy, eruption, or silence the next day might bring. Hyperdocumentation kept me indefinitely occupied and functioned as a temporary residence of ideas, grades, accolades, and presentations that kept me safe from the emotions I avoided. In the book mobile in Hilltop Green (my childhood neighborhood), I literally had a mobile library that was always there to rescue me and provide cover from the rain. At home, academic-related chores served as an escape hatch from my familial troubles. I could always say that I needed to go to the mobile library which would visit our neighborhood three times a week (as part of an outreach program) and hide out there in the company of infinite books and a soft-spoken librarian. My scholarship was my ticket out of a house full of pain, duality, religion, and strictness. I used it to my every advantage. I would check out books about all sorts of topics, sometimes reading things that I knew would be forbidden at home. At school and in the library, I indiscriminately learned about whatever was available in the bookshelves and hid in my own intellectual space.

On January 25, 2017, *The New York Times* magazine featured a story entitled "The Only Way to Fight Back is to Excel," chronicling one undocumented student's struggle to find agency in her undocumented status. It instantly resonated with me. This sentiment was also clearly reflected throughout the students' stories. In the absence of rights that citizenship brings such as driving, voting, financial aid, access to public benefits, bringing family members to the United States, the ability to travel, becoming an elected official, working at government jobs, and showing patriotism, the only way to fight back against being undocumented, and in my case, against feeling the pain of home, was to excel in school. Excelling in school, even amidst everything that tells us otherwise, is still the primary vehicle, imagined or real, to the American Dream. We have so incorporated the American Dream that plain facts are futile against the power of our desires, as impossible as they may seem.

What undocumented students have taught me is that in order to live, we must have an agentic space to cultivate an empowering self-identity. James Baldwin said, "I can't be a pessimist because I am alive." I suppose our undocumented students can't be pessimists either because their lives and often those of their families depend on optimism. In order to get through the day, the hour, the minute, the present moment is all they have. Even if seemingly unreachable, the license to vigorously dream is perhaps the only necessary ingredient to harness the energy to keep moving forward.

Undocumented students have performed the role of infallible non-citizen citizen to acquire an official citizenship status which they will never be sure to get. As I discussed in earlier chapters, citizenship is an elusive term that is used in a variety of ways. Even if they have performed good citizenry, what protection does that buy? Last year, I would have said education was the last hope, the only hope for claiming worthiness of American citizenship. This year, I can't say the same thing. It seems that education feels more like a distraction from the real possibility of deportation, like a holding pattern until you can figure out what comes next. I guess one of the things we need to ask ourselves is how is the process of schooling and the earning of educational degrees complicit in advancing unjust notions of citizenship? By encouraging our undocumented students to become further documented, are we simply perpetuating or engineering a new batch of non-citizen citizens who will domesticate their bodies and minds to the demands of hegemonic indoctrination? How are we promoting critical thinking and revolutionary action among our students if they are being trained in the same institutions that squash such behavior? In other words, what are we teaching undocumented students about what it means, what it costs, what it takes to be an American citizen? What is the hidden curriculum of hyperdocumentation?

In the next section, I revisit each aspect of the borderland love ethic by reconnecting my own personal experiences as once undocumented to now hyperdocumented immigrant to those of the participants.

BORDERLANDS AND MESTIZA CONSCIOUSNESS WITHIN A PROVISIONAL SPACE

The first aspect of the borderland love ethic discusses Anzaldúa's notion of borderlands and the mestiza consciousness required to claim all parts of one's identity within a provisional space constructed with one's own feminist architecture (Anzaldúa 1987).

Undocumented students wait in a provisional space. What we have seen here, however, is that rather than waiting in a frustrated purgatorial place, undocumented students claim all parts of their identities using their own architecture. In carving out an agentic space of hyperdocumentation, their ending place doesn't hold as much import as the process by which they arrived there. In other words, I see these students on a path toward a life of integrity, righteousness, and social justice. Whether that path leads them to American citizenship or another circuitous route to an unknown destination, their efforts are not futile. As we fight to create policies that are humane, progressive, and morally right, hyperdocumented undocumented students fashion figured worlds of academic achievement, social justice activism, and spiritual uplift.

ARMED LOVE

The second aspect of the borderlands love ethic involves hooks' (2000) and Darder's (2003) reconceptualization of love as an "armed" love that is global in its vision, intimately engaged with the collective good, and oriented toward the continual process of self-actualization.

What this process has taught me is that research can be, perhaps, should be, an act of love. In the introduction, I began by questioning my role as an academic, why I do the things I do. What academia allows us to do is to arm ourselves with a kind of official knowledge capital. It gives us a platform to validate stories that may otherwise remain invisible or silenced. When we, as researchers, engage in the kind of research that serves the collective good, we inevitably become more self-actualized. This is because doing good always requires a certain level of vulnerability, change, and reflexivity. Our local work is global in its vision if we believe that the ripples of our work indeed extend far beyond our imaginations.

Being armed with academic ammunition including the privilege of publishing our writing, teaching coursework, engaging in research, and presenting our work holds a distinct power. To participate in knowledge production and dissemination is an immense responsibility and one that I embrace and appreciate each day. Part of the borderland love ethic is an acknowledgment and commitment to this activity as part of a broader intersectional fight for social justice, done at a local level but understood as a contribution to a global effort. While the research itself is of clear importance, the process of self-actualization as researcher is equally if not more important. From my perspective, the potential transformation that research allows for the researcher to undergo should be central to our academic pursuits. The extent to which we are willing and able to change seems proportional to the extent to which our research can impact others. Like a tree, our growth depends upon our ability to shed our bark—to soften, loosen, and shed layers, boundaries, and defenses to make room for our healed, renewed, and strengthened skin. Research should not distance us from ourselves. It should bring us closer to our authenticity. In turn, that authenticity makes us more humane, connecting us to every aspect of the research process.

INTERACTIONALITY

The third aspect of the borderland love ethic is Chavez' (2013) notion of interactionality that builds on the critical concept of intersectionality (Crenshaw 1991) as "a form of rhetorical confrontation that begins critique from the roots of a problem or crisis and methodically reveals how systems of power and oppression interact with one another in ways that produces subjects, institutions, and ideologies and that enable and constrain political response" (p. 51)

As we look at the root of the problem of undocumented students and the burden of hyperdocumentation, we see the systems of power and oppression at play. We have a group of students who want to do well, want to contribute to society, and want to succeed yet the schooling process itself serves as a mythological stepping stone to citizenship while simultaneously constraining political response. In the process of schooling, we reward docile bodies that stick to the rules, achieve academically, and lay low. The conundrum of such a contradiction is that in the process of schooling undocumented students, they learn that American Dreams are built on a foundation of often subtle, sometimes overt, acquiescence to the institutions and ideologies that at once promote draconian immigration policies and perpetuate the myth of meritocracy. Sure, undocumented students can wait in a loose limbo with the hope of one day achieving an officially "safe" immigration status, but their fates are always at the whim of the political establishment of the day.

Undocumented students also embody intersectional and often marginalized identities including but not limited to age, physical ability, sexual identity, gender identity, religious or spiritual affiliation, socioeconomic class, first language, and national origin. The interaction of these identities can constrain undocumented students from engaging politically at any level out of multiple fears of persecution. In other words, being undocumented is one of many intersectional identities that influence students' decisions to act agentically. While this book primarily focused on one dimension of these students' overall identities, it is critical for future research to tend to both individual identities and their intersections to reveal the complexities that they face.

ENGAGING THE BORDERLAND LOVE ETHIC

A borderland love ethic must engage three tenets: (1) nurturing our space to love in spaces of contention, (2) tolerance of ambiguity as a revolutionary virtue, and (3) humbly beginning anew, again and again.

It is possible to engage a borderland love ethic by nurturing our space to love in contentious times under seemingly hopeless circumstances. We are reminded that love is far more than a romantic concept. Love is that fire that burns relentlessly amidst adversity. Love is the stuff of will when everything precious has been ripped away. Love is believing in times of disbelief. We have seen the ways that undocumented students nurture this space of love amidst uncertainty, persecution, and loss. They have nurtured this love with resilience and persistence even in the face of limbo.

Ambiguity is part of the human condition and will always be with us—the revolutionary aspect of our work is maintaining critical hope under such circumstances. Undocumented students who utilize hyperdocumentation as a tool of resistance and survival demonstrate this critical hope in a revolutionary way by exploiting the very system that deems them "illegal." They work the educational system to test the American Dream hypothesis, calling its bluff, and through their actions, asking: is the American Dream a dream, a nightmare, or something else altogether? The ambiguity that undocumented students face will remain a permanent characteristic of their existence. As history has taught us, immigration policies and enforcement are as fleeting as political administrations are inconsistent.

Finally, I go back to a saying that my mama always was quick to remind me of, "we are always arriving." Like the undocumented students I have had the distinct honor of working with, we must focus on the journey because the truth is that we never conclude. Undocumented students, in their quest for citizenship, understand that while citizenship may be the goal, they must focus on the process. The everyday acts of agency are not futile even if citizenship fails to materialize. As researchers, we also have to humbly begin again and again. This means that we readjust our research focus if the participants' experiences call for that. This means that, on our most frustrating writing days, when impostor syndrome rears its powerful head, we forgive ourselves and just do the best that we can in that moment. This means that when our work is rejected by another journal, we take it as an invitation to revise and resubmit somewhere else. This means that humility must be given its due worth. For me, humility in academia is about three things: (1) understanding that the importance of your work can only be measured by its ability to enact agency in its readers, (2) quietly listening to that instinct that knows what to do in moments of indecisiveness, and (3) not taking yourself so seriously that ego becomes the central motivation of the work. Academic humility, however, does not equate to meekness. We must enact agency within our own contexts. One of the most powerful ways we can do this is by writing ourselves into academia.

WRITE YOURSELF INTO ACADEMIA

Undocumented students are perhaps one of our best models and inspirations to engage in writing ourselves into academia. Their hunger for documentation reminds us of the great privilege that we have to share our words, openly and freely. Their fierce determination ignites our resolve to document what others cannot. Their strategic creativity pushes us to tell our truths in engaging and deliberate ways. More than anything, undocumented students tell us that in the face of seeming futility, the only way to survive and thrive is to commit ourselves to the moment we find ourselves in, precisely because of the uncertainty that lies in front of us. My hope is that this book inspires in these ways. In this brief final chapter, I step outside of the research articles, the academese, and the conventions of academic writing to encourage you to write yourself into academia.

What does it mean to write ourselves into academia? It means that we are allowed to take up space. We do not need to shrink. We are not alone. Someone is waiting to connect to our stories. Our stories are waiting to be told. When we write ourselves into academia, we will encounter pain in the process but we need not suffer, holding on to a gone past or clinging to an unknown future. The pain comes from unearthing, viewing, making meaning of, and then revealing what is raw and rigorous, effectively communicating our insecurities, struggling through the isolation that comes with writing, and engaging data with intensity, all toward a socially just end. The suffering emerges when we focus on expectations that were never met or are presumably on the horizon. Writing ourselves into academia requires breaking rules now by crossing the threshold from academic conventions into human emotions. This requires us to know the conventions well—twice, three, four times as well as the next person. It also requires that we set the highest of bars when it comes to the rigors of truth telling and knowledge production.

I have written myself into academia by both studying those with an identity I once shared and by using my reflexivity, personal narrative, and vulnerability to unapologetically produce knowledge that is not necessarily original as we would like to believe but perhaps new to the written word due to the educational, socioeconomic, and cultural privileges that have facilitated my ability to use text as a vehicle. In other words, this "original" knowledge is as original as immigration itself. Certainly, I am not the first to verbalize this knowledge but I have been granted license, through a variety of hazing rituals, peer-reviewed competitions, and pedigree, to present it as a book. To write oneself into academia, one has to tell a truth, ethically and daringly, with the firm knowledge that it is a process that involves a multitude of nuanced skills—a sharp command of language, a respectful understanding of those that have paved the way before us, and a vulnerability that opens you up to critique, ambiguity, and love. It is writing with fear staring you right in the face and understanding that you are not the first nor will be the last to feel afraid of putting it out there.

I began this book by sharing that my personal life and academic life are inextricably intertwined. So are yours. Academic experiences are merely manifestations of what we have been taught to believe about society, knowledge, and ourselves. They allow us to exert agency by resisting against its structures, remaining invisible within its many cracks, or working within the educational system to establish a sense of validation in our histories and lives. This may or may not be an epiphany for you but regardless of the extent to which this rings true, I want to tell you that there is more of you that needs to be written into academia. It is true—my need to hyperdocument persists. As undocumented students have taught me, hyperdocumentation may not be the ultimate antidote; it may even feed a dream deferred, but, for now, it is what keeps me critically hopeful and, whether real or imagined, safe.

REFERENCES

Anzaldúa, G. (1987). *Borderlands: La frontera – the new mestiza.* San Francisco: Aunt Lute Books.

Chavez, K. (2013). *Queer migration politics: Activist rhetoric and coalitional possibilities.* Chicago: University of Illinois Press.

Crenshaw, K. W. (1991). Mapping the margins: Intersectionality, identity politics, and violence against women of color. *Stanford Law Review, 43*(6), 1241–1299.

Darder, A. (2003). Teaching as an act of love: Reflections on Paolo Freire and his contributions to our lives and our work. In A. Darder, M. Baltodano, & R. D. Torres (Eds.), *The critical pedagogy reader.* New York: Routledge.

Gonzales, R. (2015). *Lives in limbo: Undocumented and coming of age in America.* Berkeley: University of California Press.

hooks, b. (2000). *All about love.* New York: First Perennial.

INDEX

© The Author(s) 2018
A. Chang, *The Struggles of Identity, Education, and Agency in the Lives of Undocumented Students*,
https://doi.org/10.1007/978-3-319-64614-5

V

Voice, 21, 29, 41, 56
Vulnerability, 2, 7, 34, 110, 111, 126, 129, 130

W

Walk the path, xi, 110, 115, 118
Whiteness, 9

Writing, viii, ix, 1–3, 6–10, 14, 17–19, 24, 42, 44, 60, 102, 121–123, 126, 128–130

Y

Youth participatory action research (YPAR), 109, 110, 113, 118

CPSIA information can be obtained
at www.ICGtesting.com
Printed in the USA
LVOW13*2322301117

558172LV00017B/426/P